ANCHOR BOOKS

INSPIRATIONS FROM THE

NORTH WEST

Edited by

David Foskett

First published in Great Britain in 1995 by
ANCHOR BOOKS
1-2 Wainman Road, Woodston,
Peterborough, PE2 7BU

All Rights Reserved

Copyright Contributors 1995

SB ISBN 1 85930 068 5

Foreword

Anchor Books is a small press, established in 1992, with the aim of promoting readable poetry to as wide an audience as possible.

The poems in *Inspirations From the North West* represent a cross-section of style and content.

These poems are written by young and old alike, united in their passion for writing poetry.

I trust this selection will delight and please the authors from *the North West* and all those who enjoy reading poetry.

David Foskett
Editor

CONTENTS

Wasted Years	Dora Murphy	1
You	Matthew Walmsley	1
I Never Got The Chance	A Chapman	2
Untitled	Karen McGiveron	3
Mother	Jane Rice	4
The Sea	Neil Barclay	4
Clogs	David Park	5
Rounding The Round	John Eccles	6
In Memory Of Amy	Andrea Radcliffe	7
Don't Plead Ignorance	R Thompson	8
I Care About The Rainforest	Scott W McKenzie	8
Open Eyed	P Wyatt	9
Our Mam	A Murray	9
Let Me Be	Liz Tena	10
Old Age	M O'Reilly	10
A Memory Or Two	Jimmy Pudding	11
The Warrior	Vikki Harker	11
Harvest Time	Catherine Hosker	12
Bluebells	Dorothy Clinton	12
Autumn	Allan Ormerod	13
A Place To Live	Irene Greenall	14
The Bully	Amy Merone	15
Rain	Gemma Ridgway	15
Oatmeal Grey	Lynda Banks	16
Green Fingers	Nancy Owen	17
My Town	G Strachan	18
Summer Comes And Goes	Clara Varey	18
It's Like/And When	Bruce Boertien	19
Twilight Dreams	Marion Pollitt	20
God	Jane Taylor	21
Lancashire Landscapes	Maureen Parker	21
Winter Pansies	Philip H Dobson	22
Fingers In The Socket	Nathan Burgess	22
Sorry I Forgot Tha Birthday	R M Salthouse	23
No More A Baby	S M Taylor	24

Viva A Deva	Andy Sutton-Thompson	25
I Wash The Dishes	Drusilla R West	25
Heritage Way	Fay Mandeville	26
Armchair Traveller	M Lewis	26
Homeless	John Farrell	27
Beauty	Maureen Noonan	28
Golborne Pride	Andy Brown	28
Where Is Home	Anna Elliott	29
Rochdale's My Town	Donna M Holt	30
Where	Kathleen Seed	31
Loving Ways	Phyllis Bromfield	31
The Giver Of Life	Glenys Lyness	32
The Rubbish Of Life	Paul Brooks	32
You Never Forget The First Time	Jean Carter	33
Grandma	Marian Dunn	34
The Grasshopper	Carla Jones	35
Untitled	Helen Ahmad	36
Society	Katherine Whiston	36
The Nag	E H Smith	37
An Innocent Wish	D L Davies	38
Thunderbolt	Marianne Reeve	38
Harvest Home	M Parnell	39
Ladder To Nowhere	Alex Southgate	39
In A Yorkshire Graveyard	Jo Casson	40
Untitled	H K Dilworth	41
Canal Ghosts	Farah Shaheen	41
Queen Of Hearts	Bill Jordan	42
TT Races	Michael Bell	42
A Day At The Chelsea Flower Show	Jill Gorman	43
Untitled	I M Finch	44
The Master Plan	Eugenie Barker	44
The Piper Of Loch Fay	Alfa	45
Reflections Of Life	Denise Clitheroe	46
The Face At The Window	N Jones	47
I Miss You	Jackie Drabble	48
Life From The Deep	Karen Henderson	48

Was I A Witch	Louise	49
Cheshire Country Lanes	Sheelagh Evans	49
Untitled	J P Armour	50
Our Boy	J A Spencer	51
Jack The Giant Killer	Gordon Mills	52
Gossip	Joanne Cowser	53
The Wind	Robert Old	53
God's Gift	Andrea Jay	54
The Hoarder	Geoff Edge	54
Kernow Evermore	Jonathan Middleton Webb	55
A Poem Of The Year	Carly Lancaster	56
Life After Life . . .	Lynda Miller	57
Civil War	Zoe-Marie Rowland	58
Inevitability	Malcolm G Crompton	59
Only A Dream	J Millington	59
Music Is For The Birds	R M Moulton	60
Imagine	Kathy Anderson	60
He	Dot Taylor	61
Verse To A Beloved Granddaughter	J Whitby	61
Our World	Barbara Boon	62
Poppies	J Morgan	62
Paradise Street	Mary Oliver	63
Sunset	D A Cannon	63
Remembrance	Winifred Wardle	64
Heartbreak	R McLeod	65
A Moment's Magic	John Hilton	66
Early Morning Frost, Ullswater	Margaret Mayne	66
World Of Love	Kevin P Collins	67
The Lamb	Jackie Pass	68
Kendal (The Auld Grey Town) And The Lakes	B Holme	69
Chips And Gravy	Tommy Warburton	70
Aroma	Eva Clucas	71
My Husband	Mandy Parker	72
Dreaming Of Puss	D Flamee	73
JM	David McShane	73

Glorious Devon	David Reynolds	74
Woodland Song	Sheila Devine	75
View From The Bridge	Richard Wallbank	76
Please Let Me In	Reece Bywater	77
I Am	K M Evans	78
The Good Old Days	Maria Farrell-Grundy	79
The Old Grey Tree	Peter Robinson	80
Candle In The Window	Lily Smith	81
Corners	Patricia Flynn	81
Three Ball Men	Barbara Trimble	82
For My Grandchildren	Maureen Harrison Riley	83
Cheshire Lines In Fifty Nine	John A Harris	83
The Box	Deirdre Armes Smith	84
She	Loren Moore	85
How Lucky We Are	Julie Taylor	86
The Elves	Chérianne Wren	87
To The Decline Of ICI's Winnington Plant	Philip Johnson	87
Progress	C Molloy	88
Escape To Tatton	Jenni J Moores	88
Country Life	Linda Cannings	89
Metamorphosis	David Glover	90
Toshiaght-Noa	J Ayres	91
Danny	Dawn Riccio	92
Going To School In Oldham - 1950's Style	Maggie Rich	93
Night Riders	Eileen Wiggins	94
Old Gas Lamps	Ken Mainwaring	95
Crime Of Fashion	Betty Lightfoot	96
Old Lancashire	E Blundell	96
Hey You!	Paul Rogers	97
Give Them The Beat	Violet M Corlett	98
Mi Joinery	John Fearn	99
The Remedy	Louise Hamilton	100
Poverty Is Ugly Son	H Warburton	101
At A Lancashire Station	Rod Nightingale	102
Just Another Council Estate	Stephen Starkie	102
Holiday Packing	K Leigh	103

The Jumper	Edith	104
Horwich Carnival Procession	Jackie Elvy	105
A Nostalgic Return To A Lancashire Dale	Bunty Aldred	106
Triathlon - The Bike	Robert Keith	106
The Railway Worker	Steven Bennett Whiteley	107
Na-Lad	H W Fogarty	108
The Shadow	Anne Cooper-Halton	108
Spellbound . . .	Jean Carter	109
Joe And Steph	Catherine Makin	110
A Victim Of The Armenian Earthquake	Joan Williams	111
Wastwater	Shelly Tomlinson	112
Mystic Meg On The Lottery Show	Deborah Casson	112
Freedom	Julia Yates	113
The Fidelity Of Faith	Mack A Duerden	114
Kids Today	Bert Horsley	115
Childhood Dreams	Emma Shaw	116
The Derbyshire Diet!	S Williamson	117
Don't Judge A Book . . .	Marianne Pilkington	118
Xmas Lament	Clare Martin	119

WASTED YEARS

Don't waste your life with wasted years
Of forgotten dreams and silent tears.
Don't spend your days in deep regret
Of songs unsung and aims not met.

You have one life, it is your time
To love, be loved and write your rhyme.
Be very sure of this - you have not long
To pen the words and sing your song.

Your verse should overflow with truths
In tune to a heartfelt beat.
To create the perfect masterpiece -
Is to live a life complete.

If we should meet when we are old
And your page is stained with tears.
I'll feel much anger in my heart
For all the wasted years.

Dora Murphy

YOU

When I write my masterpiece
You will be in it
It will be a poem about beauty
And you are the limit
I hope our palms will meet
And never cross
Yet my hopes brings fears
When just your motions
Can move me to tears

Matthew Walmsley

I NEVER GOT THE CHANCE

Acting seemed like second nature
Success followed him in his career
But tragedy followed him in private
Lost his wife and lost his son
Little boy playing on the river
I never got the chance to tell him
Just how much I loved him
On the day the news came through
He'd gone
Left me broken hearted
Thinking of the times
I'd seen him here
The cancer followed
And destroyed him
Wanted to be forgotten
By all his fans
It took his life
And left a widow
How I cried
The day the news came through
He'd gone
He taught me
Never to quit
When the odds were down
And gave me the strength to see
The hard times through
Just can't forget his spirit
Lives here
In the land he loved
Where dreams come true
Had to come and tell him . . .

A Chapman

UNTITLED

The dogs are barking,
But I am happy,
I'm blossoming in the sun.
The drums are drumming,
The pipes are piping,
Creeping thoughts are occurring and stirring up.
Jail, jail, all locked up,
The hand on my shoulder,
The words whispering in my ear.
The sentence in your mind,
Death, death, death,
Cold, black air.
People crying, win a race.
Got to keep moving, got to keep moving,
Move, move, move.
A blank mind, a blank head as you shudder in your bed.

At night in bed your dreams are ahead,
A tank full of water, and there at the bottom lies you
You're dead!
Frightening thoughts!
Can't sleep.

But then comes a light, a lovely bright light,
The jail door opens, you are set free,
Happy, happy, like a bumble bee.

Dancing and dancing 'til dawn.

Karen McGiveron

MOTHER

She swells
Bursting with love
Hope encaptured
Contained for just a while
Growing and forming
Hidden in bliss
Warm and content
Free inside another
Still photograph of life . . .
. . . positive negative of the future

Jane Rice

THE SEA

The sea is like a wolf hunting for food,
He's in a very bad mood.
He howls everywhere in his shiny coat of gleaming hair
Hunts for his prey.
It catches something everyday -
Apples he hates, meat he loves.
But most all (up above) he loves the smell of bacon well
He howls at night.
(And people living near get a fright.) He rests at night
In May or June.
But when winter comes (pretty soon)
He crashes the earth and makes it shake.
He jumps across the pure blue lakes.
He gnaws the bones and slashes the snow
He rolls around the Arctic pole.
He's *Big* and *Huge* and always well fed
He always stuffed and going to bed
It's turning in to June, snuggle up Wolf.
This is called the wolf rhyme
I will see you another time.

Neil Barclay (9)

CLOGS

You waited for the shoes to come 'til clogs stopped calling round
So you couldn't really credit it when he stamped on your ground.
A classless hero from the Grammar school with suits and shoes galore,
A solicitor, a sportsman and a man with so much more,
A king who had the common touch, a drinker with the boys
Who laughed the last and loudest above all competing noise.

Your wedding day was clear and cold and just before the spring
Monopolised by his obvious friends who did the obvious things,
Flirting with the bridesmaids in their pretty pastel hues
Breaking wind inside the church and sniggering in the pews.
Then streamers, cans and telegrams and screaming simple songs
A day of joy and happiness to last your whole life long.

So now you have the family and such a lovely home,
Just a bit of status and a car you call your own.
You've joined a little circle who meet each other week
To share a cup of coffee and to have a guest to speak.
It's nice to meet acquaintances when he's out earning fees,
Working such unsocial hours with a special gift to please.

Often you feel lonely but he has it all to do,
Clients who are difficult then public meetings too
And it would be rather selfish if you thought his charm and wit
Should be for you alone and not be spread around a bit.
You can well appreciate he's every right to think -
That after all the work he does, he's earned himself a drink!

So whilst he's pleasing others with his practised cheeky smile
You sometimes have a visitor of quite a different style.
With children in the primary school from nine 'till nearly five
A pair of clogs comes making sparks upon your concrete drive.
There's laughs and shouts in vulgar tongue as he kicks down your door,
A lovely rough and ready boy who throws you on the floor.

David Park

ROUNDING THE ROUND

Take the steps that rise into the stone foothills
Flagged by the worn worries of heavy leather
Relentlessly pounding the weight of yesterday
Into the potholes of tomorrow

This coiled serpent always rounding the round
With cold curved corners snaking ahead
Snapping the fortress shut as the fangs devour the scaly tail
In some secret spot

Hissing gently as pot-bellied tourists prod the rough skin
With podgy sticky fingers

Rattling to the clatter of commuters
Heads bent in silent worship
Recollections of Radio One

While soaring above in timeless majesty
The old cathedral steals the sky
Flirting with the sun in a wink of stained glass

And the wriggling walls hum to her voice apart
Clear sweet bells of Christendom locked in their sharp new tower

While the iron-laced clock whirls away another day over the teaming Eastgate
And the rounding continues to round

To the river and back
In a flash just like that
And nobody sees it move

Until the shadows creep on board
Cloaking the cricketers green and washing Charlie's spytower
In a black ether

As the phantoms play
That's when the stones waltz
To the flickering music of the moon
To the river and back

John Eccles

IN MEMORY OF AMY

He broke the mould when he made you,
In your coat of navy blue,
With matching hat upon your head
One look from you, and enough said,
Your character it was unique,
As you meandered down the street,
And at the village you would stop to
Catch a bus to visit shops,
The only ones you'd patronise were
Second-hand you got good buys,
Then weighted down with heavy load
Back home you'd come up Whitworth Road,
You'd alter this and let out that cause
Making fit you had the knack,
And when the next week came around
You'd catch the bus straight back to town,
Until the spare room creaked and
Groaned with plastic bags all strewn around
But now you've left this earthly race
It seems a large and empty place
For people like you are hard to find,
You were unique in your short time.

Andrea Radcliffe

DON'T PLEAD IGNORANCE

Drugs in our lives, not so far away
On the doorsteps where our children play
Violence and Aids, not necessarily gay
It's the scourge of mankind, here to stay.
        Where does the blame lie?
        Why does it matter?
        Coiled up in beaurocracy
        Whilst our lives are in tatters.
Wars, disease and deprivation
Are now upon our once great nation
The answer is there, can't you see
The world must change, even you and me
Our voice is the power of second chance
We must stop pleading ignorance.

R Thompson

I CARE ABOUT THE RAINFOREST

Mystical, monstrous masters roam the rainforest,
In bright colours of the rainbow, which flood the rainforest far and wide,
Trees like giant umbrellas with spaghetti-like roots,
The raindrops off the trees create sounds that man has never heard,
Howl . . . Squark . . . Hiss . . . Roar!

No trees, no scenery,
No flowers, no beauty,
No animals, no noise . . .

Who wants this environment to change
I certainly don't
I care about the rainforest.

Scott W McKenzie

OPEN EYED

His eyes are blind, he cannot see
the green grass or the stately tree
he lives in dreams of by-gone days
and doesn't understand always
why then is he 'oh' so wise
this man with the unseeing eyes
he sees much further than I or you
his faith is ever strong and true
he only knows what God above
can achieve with trust and love
he hears the birds as they sing
and thanks the Lord for everything
while we can only see the shame
and wonder where to put the blame
for war and famine everywhere
someone needs to show they care
if only we could be as wise
as he who stands so open eyed.

P Wyatt

OUR MAM

A lady was my mother, Kathleen was her name. We called her Mam,
Not mother, because from, Liverpool we came.
We never had fine riches, or toys or bikes, or such, but love
She gave us plenty, of which she had so much, she had no
Jewels just a little gold band.
To pawn on a Monday, her bare left hand.
But back on a Friday the gold band would go
On the left hand of the lady that we all loved so.

A Murray

LET ME BE

Let me be your friend for life
Marry me - I'll be your wife
Let me be your saving grace
I'm the one who has the faith
Let me be your favourite toy. . .

Let me be your eyes
See through all the lies
Let me be your hands
Building on our plans

Let me be your light
In never ending night

Liz Tena

OLD AGE

Can't put the heat on
        Can't pay the bill
Eighty years old
        And over the hill
I get a pension
        It's never enough
Can't pay my food bill
        Life's very tough
Fought in the war
        No-body cares
I even struggle to get up the stairs
        Can't sleep at night
Can't even cry
        Please leave me alone
And, just let me die

M O'Reilly

A MEMORY OR TWO

Of gaslight shadows and weavers clogs wending,
The smell of gas-tar on cobbled roads mending.

The clang of milk churns on horse drawn floats,
Of broken biscuits and penny lucky bags, childish hopes.

The burning coal on blackleaded grates,
Of slopstones filled with dirty plates.

Of swings from gaslamps; never mind the falls,
The swelling will go down with butter balls.

The smell of goose grease on one's chest,
Mum will swear it is the best.

Donkey stone on doorstep edge.
To keep the devil out it's said.

Christmas is coming, mothers dread,
What to put in the stockings at the end of the bed.

Apple, orange, maybe a little toy too,
Whatever it is it will have to do.

Jimmy Pudding

THE WARRIOR

Sensual eruptions awakened from a deep slumber.
Entranced and encaptured from deep within the soul.
Yet the warrior returns from a much needed sleep.
Prepared and relaxed enough to attain ultimate goals.
The perusal of events enlightens my senses.
The spark of life is metamorphosising into a furnace of feelings
Which will enable my immortal coil to reach my destiny,
Which I will create and design myself.

Vikki Harker

HARVEST TIME

Harvest time, harvest breeze
Leaves are dropping off the trees
Winter comes and Winter goes
The wind just howls when it blows
Crops of fruit, potatoes and jam
These were made by woman and man

Harvest season of the year
Fox, mice, rabbit and deer
Harvest is a time for sharing
Harvest is a time for caring
Conkers dropping off the trees
Followed by the Autumn leaves

Clocks go back, colours change
Potatoes stored in a range
People start to pickle things
This is what our Harvest brings
We're here in church so listen and pray
We thank you God in every way
We thank you dearly for your love
For all the things that are from above.

Catherine Hosker

BLUEBELLS

How lovely are the bluebells nestling underneath the trees,
Oak and birch and lilac, all blend so beautifully.
The butterflies, the wasps and bees visit every tiny bell
To gather up the pollen and pollinate the dell.
As rabbits, badgers, hedgehogs and other creeping things
Crawl through leaf and foliage - maybe the bells will ring!

Dorothy Clinton

AUTUMN

The leaves are slowly falling, as Autumn comes around;
    They swirl in little flurries to cluster on the ground.
We feel a tinge of sadness as the trees turn dark and bare;
    Remembering all the beauty that once was clustered there.

The wind has gathered coolness, a nip is in the air;
The rose trees look quite ragged, with odd blooms here and there.
    Swallows gather round in flocks, anxious to be away,
    For tropic climes, where sun is warm, to return another day.

The leaves in dying take the hues of glorious Autumn shades;
    Yellows, browns, and golden tints, go marching down the glades;
    And woods once clothed in living green, now wear a jester's gown;
    And as the rough wind bends the boughs, the leaves keep
                                                drifting down.

They form a carpet on the ground, and children laugh and play;
    Kicking them into ragged heaps, then scattering them away;
    And housewives busy with the brush, pretend an angry face;
    Chasing leaves and children, and losing in the race.

The falling leaves remind us, our life has reached its span;
    From the sweet bud of childhood, to when we become a man;
    The quiet years of Autumn, when the leaf fades on the branch;
    Can be blest with contemplation, and the twilight years enhance.

The falling leaf is not the end, in nature's grand rotation;
    The tree that stands so grim and bare, is awaiting new creation;
We know for sure when Winter ends, and birds begin to sing;
    New buds will bloom, glory return, and once again it's Spring.

Allan Ormerod

A PLACE TO LIVE

'You live in Lancashire, what a place?
'Tis certain I wouldn't show my face,
In its dark, damp streets, all drab and mean,
I can tell from old photos I have seen.

'Shabby people in shabby dress,
About the place I couldn't care less,
Where it rains and rains every day,
I'd be glad to get away.'

'How wrong can you be,' I replied,
I think I know what you'll decide,
When you've explored this beautiful county,
Where nature has been lavish with her bounty.

'Forward looking with modern trends,
A place where you'll make lots of friends,
People smiling and laughing, with hearts of gold,
Surely, of their kindness you've been told.

'Quiet places where you can sit and rest,
Amongst fine scenery that is the best,
Excitement too, in seaside places,
You can see the pleasure on everyone's faces.

'River banks where you can lounge and fish,
Doze in the sun as long as you wish,
Roam the moors where witches did live,
A spine-tingling moment these trails will give.

Lancashire is the place that beckons to me,
When away, I pine to see,
The old, familiar, lovely places,
The county that my heart embraces!'

Irene Greenall

THE BULLY

She threatens to punch,
She threatens to kick,
She talks to me as if I'm really thick.
But at the end of the day I don't care,
She can threaten to push and pull at my hair.

I stand in the playground at the end of the day,
Listening to what bestfriends have to say.

She stands on her own,
Now she's all alone,
She even threatened to have me a fight,
I hope because of this she has a sleepless night!

Amy Merone

RAIN

The rain is blue,
It's in my shoe,
It's in the sky,
Very very high,
It comes at night,
When it is light,
Sometimes in the day,
Especially in May,
When I am out,
It begins to shout,
I'm going to rain,
But not in Spain.

Gemma Ridgway (10)

OATMEAL GREY

Have you ever stopped to think,
what it would be like, without cement!
No tower blocks to pull down.
After they spend thousands to build them up
it cost millions
to pull them down.

All our homes would be made
of brick and stone, as they are laid.
No oat-meal grey,
for our eyes to see
Just lovely stone and a odd brick for me.

But, without cement
there would be
no little gnome fishing for his tea
for you see,
he is made of this, oat-meal cement,
this poor little gnome
fishing for his tea!

Lynda Banks

GREEN FINGERS

Another year in that allotted pitch
And those busy fingers just starting to itch,
Who love the feel of nature so much,
Eager to work and thrive in everything they touch.
But first the gentle touch of springtime
With all things bright and beautifully combined,
When Spring is in the air and plants begin to stir and worm
Their heads through the soil which has laid dormant and firm,
All through the winter days, some frosty some snowing,
The dark days gone and the sunlight now showing,
Drawing those little shoots up out of their hibernation
Adding colour to the countryside and all God's Creation.

The Universe in Spring time so fresh and clean
The start of the gardener's annual scene,
Those fingers so green are set into motion
Tilling and hoeing, then watering with a fertilised potion
The various seeds for early crops
Carefully sown on each prepared little plots,
Hoping to be rewarded perhaps by winning a prize
At the horticultural show, all grown to the exact size.
The satisfaction of this process is a wonderful feeling
To anyone who loves nature which helps and in keeping
With the regular nursing and inspection of each seed,
Eventually materialising into plants steering clear of the weeds,
And at the end of the day after spending many happy hours
Producing a good harvest and a festival of flowers,
Also thanking the good Lord for the yield
And everything grown in His own big field.

Nancy Owen

MY TOWN

Colne is a little town upon a hill,
The only place my restless heart
can ere be still.

I've wandered all over Europe's
Beautiful coasts,
But still Colne is the town
I love the most.

The Via Veneto in Rome is
Quite fine
But the streets of Colne
are first in line.

Canada is beautiful in the fall,
But if I couldn't come back to Colne
Then I wouldn't go at all.

G Strachan

SUMMER COMES AND GOES

I hear children's laughter in my ear
I think that summer's getting near;
I feel the warmth of the sun,
I think that summer has begun;
I see the clouds and rain departing,
I think that summer is now starting;
I smell hot barbecues in the air,
I think that summer is now there;
I see the leaves falling to the ground
So I'll wait for next year
To come around!

Clara Varey (13)

IT'S LIKE/AND WHEN

A happy story, with a sad, sad end,
It's like a child's, imaginary friend,
And when that friendship starts to wane,
It's like the cloud, without the rain,
And when the cloud leaves the sky,
It's like a stream, that's parched and dry,
And when the stream re-fills, and flows,
It's like the mountain peaks, with snow,
And when the snows begin to fall,
It's like a man who knows it all,
And when that man grows old, and dies,
It's like the truth, without the lies,
An when the truth is never said,
It's like a poem that's never read,
And when that poem does not rhyme,
It's like a life, on borrowed time,
And when the time, becomes the past,
It's like the love that cannot last,
An when the love forgets the deed,
It's like the blind that cannot read,
And when the blind regain their sight,
It's like the sunshine after night,
And when the sunshine gives off heat,
It's like a heart without a beat,
And when the heart will not mend,
We're back to the beginning and the sad, sad end.

Bruce Boertien

TWILIGHT DREAMS

Whilst sitting thinking after tea
I thought of all things dear to me
My husband reading evening news
Passing comment, stating views
Son was reading about motorbikes
Which to have of ones he likes
Dog is snoring in front of fire
These are all that I desire.

I'm quite contented all in all
To watch the evening shadows fall
Tomorrow is another day
When workers work and children play
I wonder what the future holds
Apart from usual winter colds
The poor and needy
Rich or greedy
Cannot alter what's in store
Be it peace or even war
Why is life so complicated

One day perhaps, though much belated
The people of the world will unite
Be they black, brown or even white
And come together in unity
Then be contented, just like me.

Marion Pollitt

GOD

God is around us, he's up in the sky,
But we can't actually see him, he's way up high.
God is my father, my saviour, my friend,
Between us there's a friendship I'm sure will not end.
For God is the thunder, the wind and the rain,
God is the sadness, the grief and the pain.
And God is also the good things we have,
And you've got to remember that all through your life.
God is the breeze, the blue sky and the sun,
God is the happiness, the gladness and fun.
For he's also the love, the care and the joy,
Which when put together makes girl and makes boy.

Jane Taylor

LANCASHIRE LANDSCAPES

Moving, moving on in time
Looking for a landscape that once was mine.
Factory chimneys, smoke and smog
Pavements echoing to the sound of clogs.
Little streets where once we played
Hopscotch, skipping, childhood games.
Hills and hollows
Places green,
Jam jars, fishing rods
Just a dream.
Quiet walks and country lanes
Gone forever nothing stays.

Maureen Parker

WINTER PANSIES

The winter pansies are on parade;
In serried ranks they're very brave.
Through Autumn breezes and Winter snow;
Their bright shining faces beam and glow.

In driving rain on frosty nights;
They close ranks and sit tight.
Blue and yellow and white and red;
Against the March winds they bow their heads.

But when the kind sun heralds the Spring,
And all the birds are on the wing;
They break ranks and blossom out,
And gaily prance and dance about.

Philip H Dobson

FINGERS IN THE SOCKET

He can only put one hand in pocket,
since he stuck his fingers 'inth' upstairs socket.
I knew that lad were up to no good,
so I smacked his rump with piece 'o' wood.
His bum glowed red,
and I sent 'im' to bed,
and he's still only 'alf learnt his lesson.
Now and again he likes t' ponder,
lettin' his fingers have a wander,
up left nostril of his nose,
fingers full t' brim 'o' rock 'ard crows
only 'arf the lesson was learnt as I said
so now he's lyin' peaceful in 'ospital bed.

Nathan Burgess

SORRY I FORGOT THA BIRTHDAY

I forgot t'send thee a card this year
An' that's not like me tha know,
But tha'll understand t reason I did
When tha 'ears mi tale of woe.

Well, last Tuesday week, chip-pan caught fire
While I were answerin' t door,
It were one o' them salesman chaps wi' a case,
Full o' brushes, an' polish for t floor.

An' on Monday morn', mi washer o'er flowed
While I were bakin' a cake,
I thowt mi feet were feelin' wet,
An' when I looked, floor were just like a lake.

Then mi better 'alf goes an' breaks 'is leg
When 'e were at work t other day,
Silly beggar fell into a dirty great 'ole
An' now we've t manage on a bit o' sick-pay.

An' burglars broke in last Thursday
While I were shoppin' up town,
They pinched mi watch and th' ol' toffee tin
In which I'd saved missel a few pounds.

An' to cap it all, this mornin'
Little Tommy, for summat t do,
Tipped a can o' paint o'er t baby's 'ead
An' now poor mites 'air is bright blue.

So tha can see as 'ow I forgot thee
An' 'ope y'll f'give mi absent mind,
Then when tha bithday comes next year
I'll send t biggest card I can find.

R M Salthouse

NO MORE A BABY

No more baby sleeping late in bed
With tousled hair and cheeks so red
No more asking for some sweets
No more secrets, no more treats
No more tiny tots TV
No more kisses just for me
No more lunches at my table
No more help when she's not able
No more stories on my knee
No more learning ABC
No more drinking nannie's coffee
No more hiding sticky toffee
No more running out to Dad
No more cuddles when she's sad
No more laughter when at play
No more a baby from to-day.
Now it's shiny shoes upon her feet,
Pretty ribbons in hair so neat
A lunch box to carry in her hand
She's heading off to unknown land
And as I walk through those big gates
An empty house for me awaits
Many said that I'd be glad
So tell me why do I feel sad
Because I couldn't break the rule
My baby's had to go to school
No more mummy's 'little mouse'
Just a lonely, empty, quiet house.

S M Taylor

VIVA A DEVA

It ceases not to amaze me of that city on a bend
The way in which they built it from top to bottom to end
Black and white wooden joists overhang with adjacent hue
With rows that must be walked along for pedestrians to view
Surrounded by Roman walls erected to protect its core
Large entrance gates were built precise at compass points all four
A water tower stands proud at one point of the wall
Which used to be a docking quay for provision and food for all
At an opposite point outside the wall an amphitheatre stands
Very popular for visitors and like as it was built by Roman hands
To a further point which you meet is a tower with a small round floor
This is noted as King Charles' view and the battle of Rowton Moor
The Cathedral with a story stands at a point inside the walls
It boasts of a brand new bell tower which often makes its calls
Outside the walls from time gone by the river course is claimed
For a famous roodee racecourse where flat races they are famed
Now to say this city is well known and not just within the North West
Is an enormous understatement as Chester it is and is best.

Andy Sutton-Thompson

I WASH THE DISHES

I wash the dishes in a dream
I make the beds
I feed the cat
I wash my bra
I drift along as on a cloud
Floating in the sunlit air
I know not what I do
For I am me
And you are you
And we're in love
      or so it seems
Until your roses don't arrive.

Drusilla R West

HERITAGE WAY

Heritage Way has much to offer,
If you wish to boost your coffer;

Recycling goods is the game,
If you want to make a name;

Magazines, newspapers, tabloid fodder,
Shredded, bedded, cows don't bother;

Canned *lifestyle*, drinks with fizz,
Your empty can is big waste biz;

Champagne, Real Ale, *cheers* in a glass,
Bottles galore . . . deposit en'masse;

Metal reclaimed, as merchants snap,
Enterprising buyers of valuable scrap;

Household items, once good news,
Rescue from skip all battered and bruised!

The past recycled, *best offer* will pay,
Waste disposal on Heritage Way.

Fay Mandeville

ARMCHAIR TRAVELLER

I've travelled miles, far and wide
From the Arctic wastes, to the Great Divide
Seen the snow-capped peak of Kilimanjaro
And have followed the trail of the wild buffalo
Fought two world wars - to hell and back
Roped the steers, with cowboy Jack
If I could remember all the books I've read
I'd never find a hat to fit my head.

M Lewis

HOMELESS

Huddled inside a green coat
Begging for money to live
A girl sixteen years of age
Have I got something to give?

Orphaned, homeless, rootless
Wander alone the city street
Cruel callous indifference
In eyes of people you meet.

Forced into fast-food houses
High prices for food and drink
Smoking relieves the boredom
Your heart is tempted to sink.

No job, roof, a vicious circle
No kindness, friendships, affection
Dignity vies with humiliation
A bid for survival, protection.

Abandoned child you were born
Suffer, cry without knowing why
For reasons not of this earth,
We wake on the day we die.

John Farrell

BEAUTY

You gave me joy, you gave me love
And love it knows no end.
You were my loyal and lovely dog
My good and faithful friend.
They say dogs don't have souls you know
But love was there to see,
And one day we will meet again
My faithful friend and me.
Because love knows no bounds
It conquers every foe,
And I loved you and you loved me
We'll meet again I know,
And what a day that's going to be
You'll greet me as before
And we'll never again be parted
As we meet at Heaven's door.

Maureen Noonan

GOLBORNE PRIDE

Town for sale but not its pride
The mine has gone men have lied.
Stay a while and feel its grit
No more men down its pit.

Town for sale wooden signs, sell the
Shops but not the mines.
I feel the heart of the humble coal,
And feel the anger of men and dole.

Town for sale the pit has gone
The shafts are filled but the
Mine lives on.

Andy Brown

WHERE IS HOME

We call many a place home for reasons unknown
is it the house you adorn or the place you were born?
Yet always home is where we live
or is it the place you grew up and played
spent idyllic childhood years so long ago
or the tumbling farm house grandad loved so
we too called it our home there was nowhere else to go.

Home then became a travelling trail
far away in a foreign land with promises at hand
when happiness was newly found in this land
a small cottage with roses by the door we found
yes this a home I could rest my soul.
The place I adore with flowers ever more
birds' song greets you in the morning light
this is our place we feel alright
not only by day also by night.

Home is where your family feel happy
sharing and caring like with like
where children can play with ease
there is only us to please
although the neighbours are a friendly lot
little in common we have got
we are available if in need
to give a helping hand indeed.

All the chattels one gathers over the years
litter your home from door to door
you do not part with them they may come in handy
or fill a gap for one of the family
if leaving home alone with familiar pieces
your heart pleases you do not feel lost
or a long way from home
until your destiny decides for you alone
wherever you will be and make a home.

Anna Elliott

ROCHDALE'S MY TOWN

Rochdale in Lancashire is the town where I was born,
  In olden days a place of cobbled streets, grimy and timeworn,
Our claims to fame are but a few,
  It's not all cotton mills and clogs (wooden shoes)
Cyril Smith is our most famous Sir,
  The biggest export out of Rochdale as it were,
Here was the start of the co-operative movement,
  A society started for its members' improvement,
Daughters of Rochdale let the world know our name,
  Gracie Fields is Rochdale's very own dame,
Another famous lass is Lisa Stansfield, a singer so fine,
  Her appearance is guaranteed to make headlines,
Lisa and Gracie lived a full generation apart,
  But both of them hold Rochdale dear to their hearts,
Even our town centre bridge is a record breaking span,
  It's the widest bridge in the world, any other becomes an also-ran,
Semi-rural, Rochdale is now the mills have gone,
  New houses and landscaped gardens; old mill land has been built upon,

Mincemeat, potatoes, carrots and onions make a Lancashire stew,
  All washed down with a good strong, sweet brew,
You'll not meet a friendlier folk,
  Great northern humour, willing to share a joke,

This is my town, where I live, work and play,
  A nice picture of Rochdale I try to portray,
Our Gothic style Town Hall is very picturesque and grand,
  It is overlooked by our Parish Church, which towers above the land,
We will not discuss the town's football team,
  They have a strong following but seem to be swimming downstream!
Not all towns have a magnetic pull for me,
  But Rochdale is my home town and always will be.

Donna M Holt

WHERE

Where near the river Wyre,
Would you like to retire,
The river as a rule,
Flows fast by Skippool,
Preesall is pleasant,
Just right for a pheasant,
Stalmine is great,
Catch a bus by your gate,
Pilling has her pride,
Hambleton in the guide,
Fleetwood nice, the ozone fishy,
Knott End class and swishy.

Kathleen Seed

LOVING WAYS

Take a look around
There is love to be found,
Take it from the heart
That will be a start,
You're a flame in my fire
My whole world's desire,
Just take me in your arms
With your loving charms,
With a goodnight kiss
I would never miss,
Off to bed with thoughts of you
Loving dreams warm and true,
Waking up to hear birds singing
Thought it was church bells ringing,
Hope this message will bring good cheer
And love to last throughout the year.

Phyllis Bromfield

THE GIVER OF LIFE

An orphan child in rags,
Tears in her eyes,
Looks up appealingly,
Then sags,
Once more to the pavement,
When all hope of help is declined.

It is this indifference to life
That is sad,
To give is better than to receive,
The most precious gift is the gift of life.

We all take it for granted, but
To carry a card is to tell others
What is wanted.

Glenys Lyness

THE RUBBISH OF LIFE

The world was born alive and glowing
Then man was born and litter started
    flowing
Card metal ash and tin where and when
    Did it all begin.
Re-cycle things don't burn them up
Because when it's all gone they'll be
    no but
Plant a seed plant a tree
Make sure there's air for me
For to live is to love so breathe
    in the bliss

But think don't sink under the rubbish
    of Life

Paul Brooks

YOU NEVER FORGET THE FIRST TIME

I'll never forget the first time
I saw the soft white snow.
Falling past my window
When I was only four.
Then riding down the hillside
With Daddy on a sleigh
The Snowman with my hat and scarf
And pipe made out of clay.

I'll never forget the first time
I saw the sunset gold.
Streamers red danced round the clouds
And then as one they mould.
Their restless ever changing shapes
Float gently o'er the sky.
'Til dusk her mantle spreads her arms
And images then die.

I'll never forget the first time
I saw a baby born.
His cry of life, eyes strain to see
The world to which he'd come.
From shelter in his mother's womb
He suckles at her breast.
The comfort of her cradling arms
Like fledglings in their nest.

Oh - I'll never forget the first time
Running barefoot through the hay
Then entwined as love we found
As beneath stars we lay.
There never can be that moment again
Never again that time -
Of love, so strong, so tender and pure
When we left our childhood behind.

Jean Carter

GRANDMA

It's nice to have a Grandma,
When Mummy's being mean.
Mummy likes to tell me off,
But Grandma's not so keen.

She always sends me presents
When my birthday comes around,
And when we go to Grandma's house,
Some treat is always found.

She takes me to the swing park,
And she takes me to the zoo,
And if my Mum's behaved herself,
We sometimes take her too.

My Grandma has a special bed
That folds up like a chair,
She keeps it ready just for me
For when we stay up there.

My Mum and Daddy have to sleep
Downstairs on the settee,
But I'm her special favourite,
So she keeps a bed for me.

My Grandad lives there too, of course,
And when Grandma's cooking tea,
We two will build a wardrobe,
Or watch snooker on TV.

There's lots of aunts and uncles too,
Who come and go all day,
And I'm their favourite nephew,
(At least that's what they say).

My Mum told me a funny thing
One day as we just sat,
She once was Grandma's little girl,
And Grandad's. *Fancy that!*

Marian Dunn

THE GRASSHOPPER

I used to have a grasshopper
it only had three legs

the others disappeared when dad
was cutting the hedge

it nearly got run over too
when mum was hoovering up

seconds away from being eaten
by next-door neighbour's pup

then the day finally arrived
and my grasshopper had died

a grasshopper's probably nothing you
think but it was everything to me

so when the news was final
I had to shed a tear

the grasshopper was lucky
I'd had it for a year.

Carla Jones

UNTITLED

In these days of men in space,
A video nation or computer race,
Where man goes forth in leaps and bounds,
To build up cities where once were mounds,
Where men and women are treated as equal,
Yet still the past has bred a sequel,
Of social class and racial wars,
That live and fester like open sores,
While people are judged by wealth or skin,
There can never be harmony felt within.

We are all the same despite our colour,
When we see past skin our lives will be fuller,
All of us bleed and all of us cry,
We all see the same moon in the same sky,
There's enough in this world for all to share,
If we stamp out hatred and start to care,
If you're black or white matters not to me,
You're a human being, that's all I see.

Helen Ahmad

SOCIETY

As we look on Society today
as we see humanity slip away
as we see people running
from the truth
hiding behind their fears
weeping empty tears.
As we look on Society
today will it always be this
way or is there a golden sunrise
Or is life just made up of
lies.

Katherine Whiston (14)

THE NAG

In the garden
I've a yen
For peaceful browse,
So plants I'll douse.

Hosepipe ban,
Thus watering can
Wielded by hand
Moistens the land.

Relaxed and calm,
Need no alarm . . .
Heck! What's that din?
Oh no, *she's* in!

Mrs Cross-Patch
Starts slanging match
And, tongue too loose,
Slings verbal abuse.

Scolding shriek,
Husband meek
Takes no more -
Wipes the floor.

Neighbours tell
'She's not well.'
'He's a saint -
White as paint.'

Should we flit
Away from it?
No, we'll cope
And live in hope

Of reformed nag
- or effective gag!

E H Smith

AN INNOCENT WISH

I watch my babies as they sleep,
My only wish, that they could keep
That innocence unique to youth
Of nothing else but good and truth.

If they could just remain naive,
And see this world as they believe
As one of love and peace throughout,
Instead of conflict, hate and doubt.

Why can't they just be *Peter Pans*
And live out dreams of childhood plans?
But no, instead they must endure
A growth of murder, bombing, war.

Still, there is no escape, I know
From this almighty horror show.
So please, just keep them safe, I pray,
To see another bloody day.

D L Davies

THUNDERBOLT

I've been struck by just one thunderbolt -
coming across you one night,
catching your eye,
realising you glowed like a host
of archangels - the sun spouting
from your every pore; you were golden
and holy with warmth and light and life.

Oh my illumination!
You were something hallowed
and very precious,

you whose light I dimmed

Marianne Reeve

HARVEST HOME

As the *chapel* bells ring
And the choir-boys sing
The country folk, gather together
In the little village church.

The colours of autumn, are *present*
From produce brought *off the land*
And flowers bedecked the quaint church
For the Thanksgiving Harvest-morn.

The crops are now safely *gather'd in*
Stored away from winter's *chills*
A bounty, from soil, and toil
And dedicated, village *folks.*

M Parnell

LADDER TO NOWHERE

From the depths of despair,
the steps of ice lead upward.
At the top there is nowhere,
nothingness and onward.

Too many silky images,
once like you and me.
Snapped up by inspirational savages,
looking for one blank effigy.

So never plan your life ahead,
you can't know how well you'll fare.
From your high hopes you'll drop like lead,
and climb the ladder to nowhere.

Alex Southgate (13)

IN A YORKSHIRE GRAVEYARD

Peacefully in her grave,
My little daughter slept,
Away from all the hate in the world,
Her memories I kept.

The light from the moon shone down,
On the carpet of white on the ground,
While bats circled around my head
I dared not make a sound.

The sound of a lone owl hooting,
Shook the peace of that night,
Its wings extended behind me
As we both seemed to take flight.

The graveyard was like an island,
Encircled by heather and gorse
The headstones stood tall and eerie,
Born from the eternal moors.

This place was somehow haunting,
Yet tranquil and at ease,
Despite the earthly scent of death
And the sound of creaking trees.

Everyone there was at rest,
Underneath the stones they lay,
Why should death be feared so much
If they lie in peace today.

Jo Casson (13)

UNTITLED

A soldier lay about to die
The glint of a tear in the corner of his eye,
A memory of his life, a picture he drew.
His family at home the joy he once knew.

And now as a veil of darkness o'er him came,
From whence came the bullet it needed not a name.
It was a soldier's lot in war to fight.
Never to question or look for insight.

This he had done without fear or favour,
But now he knew his life was ne'er over
A tear down his cheek it gently rolled
His breath within, he could no longer hold.

H K Dilworth

CANAL GHOSTS

Through every limb the green rot seeps,
Of their barge, into the unfeeling silence creeps.
They have seen a million faces,
Yet their shadowless eyes bear no traces.

The presence of their still souls brood
Crumbling as dust through the cracks
                                  in the wood.
A weary mother in her loneliness
Presses her frost shrivelled children in empty caress.

The rheumatic creak of old dreams and echoes
Wander sightlessly each woeful night,
Beyond the last lock their hovel barge goes
In the fitful shroud of the moon's white light.
An empty skull, in the trick of the light.
Past the throw and tug of the canal trees
Limps the coughing old barge which nobody sees.

Farah Shaheen

QUEEN OF HEARTS

they came unexpectedly
dressed in a strange darkness,
hunting you,

with double-barrelled guns
and half-starved dogs
and devices to detect fear.

for no nights and two days
they tortured your name,
but to no avail.

I told them nothing
from burst lips
and cut-out tongue.

how could I tell them
you are a living flame
burning deep in my heart.

Bill Jordan

TT RACES

The TT Races are made for the aces,
With Joey Dunlop on top.
The people drinking beer.
Have got no fear.
So they hardly ever stop.
The people give cheers.
Bikes turn to faster gears.
Some people end up in tears.
The chills.
The thrills.
And the spills.
Happy faces.
The TT Races.

Michael Bell (11)

A DAY AT THE CHELSEA FLOWER SHOW

A carpet of colour, so stunning and bright
A gardener's dream, a wonderful sight
Fuchsias, pansies, roses in bloom
Breathtaking beauty, dispelling gloom.

The planting formation, a touch of flair
The aroma of scents, fills the air
Lush green lawns, so expertly mown
Thriving so well, from the finest seeds sown.

Petite pots, to dynamic displays
Oozing splendour, day after day
Delicate blossoms that tickle your nose
Lingering perfume, from a sweet smelling rose.

Dazzling daffodils colour the earth
Standing so bold, in all their worth
Fragrant flowers, in abundance abound
Like the Garden of Eden, paradise found.

Pretty plants, baskets so bold
Small dainty buds that yearn to unfold
Climbing ivy, that reach for the sky
Magnificent conifers, incredibly high.

All tended with love in the summer sun
Bringing endless enjoyment to everyone
Setting such standards, so seldom seen
No greater show, has there ever been.

Ensuring this day will always last
Not just becoming a memory that's past
Captured on film, an experience to treasure
The magic of Chelsea, and all of its pleasure.

Jill Gorman

UNTITLED

Life is important we all agree
As each day dawns we long to be free
To take it in both hands and to say
It's my life that counts and then we pray
Are we making the best of living
Do we enjoy the pleasure of giving
The feeling of fulfilment as each day closes
Looking forward to tomorrow though it may not be roses
The sky may be grey, the sky may be blue
The sun may shine right down on you
Things may go right, things may go wrong
Life will be brighter if we greet it with a song.

I M Finch

THE MASTER PLAN

God has got a master plan,
To guide and guard this world of man.
In lands where there is stress and strife,
He to them all, will bring new life.

Sometimes the way is dark despair,
But God in Heaven is always there.
And Jesus came on earth to live,
A new commandment there to give.

Love your neighbours, love them well,
The power of love, no man can tell.
As the years come and go,
Peace will return to earth below.

For all the stars in space above,
Were made by God in His great love.
Dear God of Heaven, earth and sea,
The Universe belongs to thee.

Eugenie Barker

THE PIPER OF LOCH FAY

O, the lady of Kilnoch
so longs
for the lone piper

he woos across Fay Loch
his lady of Kilnoch
the lone piper

her love is deep
his strong as the rock
around the castle of Kilnoch

o, how the laird curses
Fay Loch
and the piper

longing, far apart
his call erodes her heart
she dies amidst the heather

he begs across the Loch
come, lady of Kilnoch
to the lone piper

and the heather on the rock
burns red
across the Loch
for the lone piper.

Alfa

REFLECTIONS OF LIFE

When we are born, our thoughts are new
They all belong to me and you.
As time goes on this all will change
We share our thoughts and dreams so strange.
As toddlers we learn behaviour and speech,
We learn not to touch the things out of reach.
When we go to school, we leave the nest
We've got to learn to be the best.
We spend our lives competing with others
Sisters trying to be better than brothers.
Then in our teens, things start to get tough,
We really try to be good enough.
To find a job and be secure
Sometimes it's tough, long hours to endure.
Relationships fail, sometimes we despair
When we least expect it, suddenly we're a pair.
The next step is marriage, we take a vow
At last we're a couple, facing anything now.
When we have children, we try to be there
To soothe all their fears, and show them we care.
When they grow up, we give them our backing,
And try to make up for things we were lacking.
Grandchildren are next, a joy to behold,
We treasure them all, tender love we enfold.
Our lives are touched with memories and sadness,
We enjoy the good, and savour the gladness.
Life's what you make it, that's what they say.
So enjoy every minute that's in every day.

Denise Clitheroe

THE FACE AT THE WINDOW

I can see you up there on the fourteenth floor
Like a fairytale Princess behind a locked door
Are you waiting like her for rescue to come
Or don't you care anymore 'cos your fingers are numb

Is this world down below too confusing for you
Are the things going on here too frightening and new
Have your old friends all left you lost and alone
Do you wish you were with them and not on your own

Do you feel the cold more with each passing day
Are the neighbours too busy to call in and say
How are you today? Have you warmth, have you food
They'd be sure of a welcome and you'd not think them rude

But nobody knocks on your door anymore
It's as if you didn't exist that's for sure
Yet I know you are there and I really do care
Perhaps if I knew you a friendship we'd share

But like all the others I'll just turn away
Yes I'll give you a thought at the end of my day
A day filled with hustle and bustle and scurry
You creep into my mind and I really do worry

For you are one of many today
Why do we treat you in this uncaring way
We should all venture up and open the doors
Of old ladies like you on those fourteenth floors.

N Jones

I MISS YOU

I miss you so much it hurts me to tell,
I don't know your touch, I've forgotten your smell,
We did all the things that lovers do,
A kiss in the rain a day at the zoo,
I'd wait by the phone all night and all day,
A very quick phone call to hear you say,
'I'm very busy I can stay on,
Meet me at the park at one.'
You said you would leave her but things got better,
You would tell her straight or leave her a letter,
It's not me who waits by the phone anymore,
It's your little girl who waits at the door,
Daddy will come just wait and see,
I don't think he's coming does Daddy love me?
All good things must come to an end,
This is one, please no more pretend,
The time has come to get a new life,
I have your daughter you still have your wife.

Jackie Drabble

LIFE FROM THE DEEP

A light is born
to the deep its formed
this grace and beauty
glides through the flow
leaping from within the sea
      let's learn how to be
So the creatures can
      stay safe
in the deep blue
untouched and true.

Karen Henderson

WAS I A WITCH

Over the years I've had many cats,
Most of them chosen by me.
But six of these cats simply moved in,
And decided my lodgers they'd be.

I have pictures of cats, ornaments too,
All of them given as gifts.
But there's one thing in common all of them have,
Which is making me wonder a bit.

Was I a witch in a previous life?
It's beginning to look that way.
For all of these cats that were given to me,
Are as black as the Ace of Spades!

Louise

CHESHIRE COUNTRY LANES

Saplings from a past decade bear their age with pride
inheritors of an inner fortitude all adversities defied.
Heads aloft these aged custodians keep watch on Country lane
shielding the weary traveller from sweltering heat and chilling rain.
Along winding lanes cool on a sultry day
dwarfed amid Nature's seasonal display.
leafy trees merge way into the distance
flanked either side they stake their stance.
Boughs meet and entwine, an archway overhead
a natural canopy with foliage outspread.
This mosaic medley of sunlight and shade
becomes a cool retreat in a twisting glade.
Travelling these tranquil trails far from milling motorway
they are a pleasing truce in the course of a hectic day
a jigsaw of shapes in a multi-hue of green
Cheshire's resplendent trees capture the scene.

Sheelagh Evans

UNTITLED

The broken maimed of Ireland, started many years ago
When someone said 'It's my land, and I will say what goes'.
The babies dead and dying, the mothers full of dread,
The men and soldiers lying, in streets of Belfast dead.
For all this war is born of hate, from parents handed down,
But, please before it is too late, let tolerance, reason crown.
The living ones and living days, of all who live in fear,
And let them end the cruel ways, let life and love be dear.
For many rights and many wrongs, have given so much pain,
So let once more the Isle of Song, bring love and peace again.
For history has nothing taught, but hate and fear and woe,
And blood that's shed has nothing bought, but tears of long ago.
A man or woman who is born, a different faith from you,
They have no need to be forlorn, a civil right's their due.
You might as well dislike a man, because his eyes are blue,
Or because his skin is tan, because he might be you.
For skin and eyes and cause and creed, may not be of your choice,
So take your place and please take heed, we don't all have one voice
So voice your preference slowly, and keep your temper low,
Remember one so lowly, so very long ago,
Who died for those who doubted him, who suffered all their pain,
Who knew their every single sin, who lived and will again.
So Ireland, blessed, bloody land, take heed and try to care,
Just give a thoughtful helping hand, and make *Him* welcome there.

J P Armour

OUR BOY

He had no words that he could say
And could only watch, the others play
He wasn't like the other boys
He could not even, hold his toys

His limbs were useless, as if of lead
And all his food, to him was fed
Sometimes within his eyes, was pain
But soon the sun came out again

A silent world was all he'd got
He never seemed to want a lot
But, as he couldn't tell us so
How were we, to really know

It made us feel so very humble
When at times, we'd start to grumble
For when we turned we'd see such joy
Upon the face, of this, our boy

We think he understood the words we said
Especially, when beside his bed we prayed
To God to give, his care and love
And always watch him from above

Now that he's gone, although we're sad
Within our hearts we're really glad
That now he's safe, and in God's care
And that one day, we'll meet him there

J A Spencer

JACK THE GIANT KILLER

Oh I feel like Jack the Giant killer in the wilderness
My mind is in a turmoil and my life is in a mess
I wouldn't face the music 'cos it was too hard to play
I couldn't stand to hold her hand and watch her fade away

There are those who could find comfort to stay and be close by
Yet I couldn't sit there on that lonely chair and see my loved one die
I don't know if she could sense it that inner howling cry
But the embracing gloom of that cold still room was no place for our goodbye

I ran out into the gardens into the clean fresh morning air
and gasped for breath like a man possessed and stared a madman's stare
There was no-one there to help her as she slipped through death's trapdoor
Beyond man's will and surgeon's skill my love would be no more

In disbelief, consumed with grief I wandered in the dawn
and cursed the shame that in life's game how man is but a pawn
My mind a flood of passions from anger to despair
As I tried in vain to ease the pain how could I leave her there?

I went in search of solace from the local parish priest
Though I'd never been one of his flock he could say a prayer at least
He said 'I wish I had the power to mend a broken heart
Or some fine words to comfort you whilst yours is torn apart
I can only say I'm sorry and know the hurt you feel
and pray that time will heal the wounds that only time can heal.'

Oh I feel like Jack the Giant killer in the wilderness
My mind is in a turmoil and my life is in a mess
I wouldn't face the music 'cos it was too hard to play
I couldn't stand to hold her hand and watch her fade away

Gordon Mills

GOSSIP

Elizabeth Walker,
Was a talker,
Chatter, chatter, chatter.
She met her friend,
They talk no end,
Natter, natter, natter.
A cup of tea,
A cream eclair,
Fatter, fatter, fatter.
'Is that the rain,
On the window pane?'
Patter, patter, patter.
The time has come,
To head for home,
Scatter, scatter, scatter.
Remember to seek,
Some news for next week,
Chatter, chatter, chatter.

Joanne Cowser (10)

THE WIND

The wind is invisible
The wind is imprisonable.
The wind can be hot.
The wind can be cold.
So anyone, who would fight
the wind, must be very bold
for he gallops upon his horse,
that can fly.
He soars across the cloudy
sky.

Robert Old (7)

GOD'S GIFT

There will be a time when man will lose
all rights God gave, our right to choose,
Our way of life will change so soon
as sure as God, created his moon,
His earth, savaged, by mindless fools
all together, we've broken all the rules,
This wonderful world, given as a gift
slowly being torn by an endless rift,
Was God so naive, to think we'd care
and keep his world, so sweet and fair,
The damage is done, the earth is bruised
God's gift was ours we wrongly used,
When that time comes and God's gift returns
it's a lesson to show, man never learns.

Andrea Jay

THE HOARDER

My Father is a hoarder, he won't throw things away,
If we try to discard them, he says they have to stay.

He saves old lengths of timber, saying they'll come in one day,
He's yet to find a use for them, but he won't throw them away.

In the shed he has three lawn mowers, a roof rack and three bikes.
A pair of ancient golf shoes, with rusty worn out spikes.

Hanging up there are three bow saws, two hoes and several rakes,
Dad says he needs to keep them all, in case one of them breaks.

He keeps old lumps of sandstone, some large and some quite small,
They just lie in the garden, in case we need a wall.

My father is a hoarder, he won't throw things away,
We want to hold a boot sale, but Father says *no way!*

Geoff Edge

KERNOW EVERMORE

Kernow's not a part of England,
nor even your *Westcountry*.
So near to being an island,
it's such a travesty.

A land of Celts and immigrants,
the latter to the fore.
I'm like a vexatious litigant,
told to sue no more.

To deny our heritage you see,
is a Saxon trick I'm sure.
Just paint us quaint and twee,
and with *Westcountry* once more!

We won't be labelled English,
of that you can be sure.
We're cousins of the Welsh and Scottish,
Cornish Britons ever more.

Onen hag oll!

Jonathan Middleton Webb

A POEM OF THE YEAR

January	Snowballs are thrown
	No flowers are grown.
February	As the days come longer
	The sunbeams become stronger.
March	It's springtime now
	Snowdrops' heads bow.
April	Little lambs prance about
	Children laugh and shout.
May	Blossoms bloom on the trees
	You hear the buzz of bees.
June	It's a sunny time of year
	You might even see a hare.
July	It's time for kites to fly
	Way up into the sky.
August	It's a time to play.
	A time to stop going away
September	Back to school again
	I'm glad my sister's a pain.
October	It finishes with Halloween
	Ghosts and witches might be seen.
November	Sparklers round the bonfire shine
	Turkeys gobble for the last time.
December	Presents come pouring in
	A loving and giving time within.

Carly Lancaster (10)

LIFE AFTER LIFE ...
(Dedicated to Florence Crozier)

Do any of us really know what life is all about?
We come into it asking questions, and the same going out,
In the race to the 'great unknown', what lessons do we need?
And are there special guardians waiting to give us that lead?

There are times in our lives when we know we are wrong
But learning from experience keeps us renewed and strong,
For none of us is perfect, it has got to be said,
And we should be breaking the negative cycles instead.

And when we are gone, we leave many others behind
With their own trials, tribulations, and life solutions to find,
Most of all we need compassion, and the capacity to forgive,
For as with food and water, they give us the strength to live.

In life, at the end of every tunnel there is light
In death, our spirit uses it, and suddenly takes flight,
We've read of the place where everything is pure and fair,
But are there truly angels, hovering to take us there?

Where do we go from here, when *this* journey is done?
We know ourselves in this life, but is there a next one?
When memories flicker, as old doors close, and new ones open,
I *know* I'll see you again, I'm just not quite sure when ...

Lynda Miller

CIVIL WAR

The former Yugoslavia
The name of a once great nation,
Ravaged now by civil war,
It's citizens soldiers - killing,
Or refugees - dead and dying,
Towns and cities lay in ruins,
Fought over by their governments,
Who seem to know or care nothing,
For so many suffering souls,
Politicians who don't know,
Of any fear for their lives,
All those children who once like me,
Would watch TV or play or read,
Now flee before so many armies,
Who now seek to kill the people,
Who were once their friends and neighbours.

How many of the refugees,
Will ever see their homes again?
Will children go to school once more?
Do the generals ever think,
Of casualties they leave behind?
When all the leaders have quite finished,
Playing their petty little games,
Will there be anybody left,
Who they'll be able to rule?
Or will the land then be covered,
With the corpses of these people,
Whose lives are to be sacrificed,
For their self-centred ruler's gain?
Does anybody really care,
What those faceless masses feel?

Zoe-Marie Rowland

INEVITABILITY

Living things can never be immune from death,
But death be immune from life, and needed.
Mourn not when yours cease from their breath,
Celebrate the creation of life, even if theirs is speeded,
Sometimes tragic, but love gave, those tears expected.

Life serves no real purpose, only to be lived,
So why disgust of one's own life taken, we are not protected.
If given no death, we would want it, for memories relived.
It is said to a better Place we will be sent,
But we may prefer the love of life than go to the Kingdom above.

Life is said to be precious, but bloodshed is still present,
Conflict still occurring, when the basis of our lives is love.
Though when it comes to my love, I will cry,
My ever fervent hope, there are no tears when I die.

Malcolm G Crompton

ONLY A DREAM

Land of hope and land of dreams,
Waving palms, where the sea creams.
Curling waves, beckoning me
To unwind, 'neath a small tree.

Sunshine smiles the live-long day,
Calling me home by the bay.
Parodies! Soft breezes blow,
Kiss the skin; Heaven, I know.

Warm, soft sand beneath the feet;
Happy time, pleasurable heat;
Where is it? Only a dream
In my mind a glitter gleam!

J Millington

MUSIC IS FOR THE BIRDS

If music be the food of love play on.
Or so the poets wrote in days of yore.
But things have changed, not for the best
This sentiment of old remains no more.
Music calmed the troubled breast so we are told
Again it was the ancients in their prime
Who wrote these words of wisdom, words of gold
And once again they're wrong, it does not work
But just evokes complaints which in their time
Can cause the magic sound to wither and to die.
Pack up your pipes, your flutes, your drums,
Accordions and organs, fiddles and guitars
Turn up the television, watch a play
And tell the world that music's had its day.
But don't believe these inconsequential words,
Just tell me who will quieten the birds.

R M Moulton

IMAGINE

Imagine a winter without any snow.
Or a spring with no trees of green.
Imagine a summer with no sun or flowers.
Or an autumn with no falling leaves.
Imagine a sky that's never blue.
Empty of birds on the wing.
Imagine a sea that's polluted and dead.
Devoid of all living things.
Imagine this earth crumbling and dying.
Its life ebbing into decay.
Imagine God looking down on the world.
On the glorious creation he made.
Then imagine his sorrow at what man has ruined.
And his tears as he takes it away . . .

Kathy Anderson

HE

He healed the sick
He cured the lame
He even rose from the dead
But still they thrust
A crown of thorns
Upon His lowly head

His love is as the driven snow
Spread throughout the land
We only have to reach out
And take it by the hand
This love is shown in many ways
Sometimes we cannot see
A love so pure and gentle
He passes on to me.

Dot Taylor

VERSE TO A BELOVED GRANDDAUGHTER

Think of me in days to come.
Remember your early years in the sun.
Now you pay a brief visit and then you go
And of each other we little know.

I planned to teach of things loved and so rare
Of books and of history and traditions that were.
Then snatched from my knee you were primed by TV
With pop groups and anarchy and hatred of rules
Believing love of country was just for fools.

Will earlier planting by me take good root
And love for nobler things bear fruit
Or has derision won the day
And stole my flesh and blood away.

J Whitby

OUR WORLD

In this world of the Nineties what has it brought
It's brought new technology space ships and sports
It's brought us great scientists with new medical thoughts
And doctors who transplant to give us new life
Modern drugs to eliminate disease that is rife
But across many countries there's still murders and crimes
Just why should this be in these modern times
Perhaps if we shared the things we don't need
By thinking of others and less of our greed
A fair distribution of the talents we've got
Would help many people especially those who have not
How nice it would be to see more jobs for the young
Love between nations no-one hungry or cold
Poverty erased and Peace for the Old.
Let us strive for this goal as the Millennium draws near
Going forward in Faith to the Twentieth years.

Barbara Boon

POPPIES

Blood red poppies for the men they miss,
Thoughts of the brave and the death they kissed.
Standing in line their heads so bold,
Thoughts of the brave that never grew old.
Friends and lovers that marched away,
Thoughts and faces never to stray.
Remembering dreams they held in their hearts,
Thoughts of a war that tore them apart.
Holding memories and letters they sent,
Thoughts of the brave that so willingly went.
A bitter sadness for a war and its graves.
Thoughts and remembrance when poppies are laid.

J Morgan

PARADISE STREET

Whippet dogs no shoes just clogs
Back to back houses in Paradise Street
Where ragged children in bare feet
On doorsteps sat in summer heat
Descriptive names, like Rose Hill
It never saw a blade of grass
Only mills and chimneys and
Mill owners making brass.
A pub on every corner with
Father drinking ale
And Mother, shawl drawn round
Her, passed by, drawn and pale.
Poverty and hunger, the yoke of
Simple folk
A life consumed by *Cotton*
They never had a Hope.

Mary Oliver

SUNSET

The sunset comes over the fells,
The birds all fly away.
An inner peace, tranquillity, sleep
Falls over the dying day.

Oh you fells, oh you sea,
Oh you magnificent lakes.
So peaceful now, so quiet, so deep
You are there for us to take

Relish the sunset, relish the views,
Absorb it into your mind.
Remember it well, when darkness falls,
Tomorrow look again - what will you find?

D A Cannon

REMEMBRANCE

Not just today we Remember,
The men who died today,
So long ago in the trenches and fields
So far away.
They gave these lives for freedom
A waste of time you say
For we are more imprisoned the way
We live today.
For the children today will never know
What it's like to stand at the door.
And watch your dad and son go away
And never return any more.
Only just a letter the edges trimmed in black
Which said in a few words
Your son's not coming back
But they say he died a hero and a medal
They will give
We didn't want the medals
We just wanted them to live.
For war can never gain anything
Just lives that were wasted away
All those thousands of sons and dads
So we could have our *today*

Winifred Wardle

HEARTBREAK

In the dimming light of a rainy morn
A sweet and tender love was born.
Crying out to be unleashed,
Replacing another that had long ceased.
Gaining strength from day to day,
Alive with energy waiting to say,
'A love for each other good and strong,
Should go on forever likes the words of a song.'
There for all the world to see, but not to touch.
My darling, I love you, I love you so much.

I want to hold you so close to me,
Say I adore you, that you'll always be
The one that I turn to when the going gets rough,
The one I will turn to when I've had enough
Of this life full of heartaches now filled with regret,
For the things that I wanted but not the courage to get.

My life seems so empty now that you are no more,
Like a room that is silent when you go through the door.
The anguish and tears that I know you have had
Must have left you with scars for which I am sad.
If, I could only take back, one year of my life,
Avoided the heartaches, the anguish and strife.
I know I have hurt you through being so weak
And pray to God for the forgiveness I seek.
The cross that I bear to my dying day,
Is knowing I've hurt you in a very special way.

R McLeod

A MOMENT'S MAGIC

Silent she sits, in concentration wrapt,
Upon the grassy sward, beneath the orchard bough,
Whilst all around the sounds of summer
Push their soft distractions to her frowning brow.

The frog, inscrutable as well befits his kind,
Impassively returns her quiet gaze
And ponders deep this strange expectant child
Whilst knowing nought of tales from olden days.

Her mother watched in fascination stilled
Her heart o'er stretched in captivated love.
She struggled hard this tableau to construe -
To grasp the hidden meaning from above.

At last she bent her knee upon the grass
The secret of this magic to evince
And heard her child in some dismay complain
'Why won't you turn into a handsome prince?'

John Hilton

EARLY MORNING FROST, ULLSWATER

Last night the winter frost crept silently,
Touching with icy fingers the lake's rim,
Painting the withered sedge with hoary rime.
White, alabaster-pale and crystalline
The reeds stand tall like silver sentinels.
Wreathed in the swirling mantle of morning,
Soft sable, argentine and misty grey,
Mirrored in wine-dark depths, the hills loom tall,
Albescent, opaline and deathly calm,
Breathing the stillness of the winter dawn.
While by the water's brim black birches trail
Witch-fingers, scarcely moving, in the lake.

Margaret Mayne

WORLD OF LOVE

God above please, look down on me.
Send down your light, so I can see.
Let me feel, your sun shining above.
Let me see, your world of love.

Let me see, your sky so blue.
Let me feel, the love from you.
Let me gaze upon, a blue moon above.
Let me see, your world of love.

Warm my heart, with love from you
Give me the feeling, of your love so true.
I whisper the name, of Jesus above.
Let me see, your world of love.

Angels above, please show me the way.
Give me the words, I want to say.
To the God above, who created all
Flowers of the valley, things big and small.

Though I'm blind, I'd love to see.
Your world's creations, you made for me
One day in heaven, with the angels above.
For the first time I'll see, your world of love.

Kevin P Collins

THE LAMB

Your life is so short little one,
Enjoy it whilst you can,
Your destiny, your certain fate,
Lies in the hands of man.

What God gave you so freely,
Man simply takes away,
Make the most of what you have,
And live for every day.

Taste the sweetness of the grass,
Feel its softness 'neath your feet,
Play and gambol with your friends,
Heed your mother's calling bleat.

Embrace the warmth of sunshine,
The gentle Summer rain,
Breathe the soft caressing air,
Here you'll feel no pain.

You'll never know what I know,
Though you will sense fear,
When man decides your time has come,
Before you've lived a year.

Your life is so short little one,
Enjoy it whilst you can,
For soon you'll die at man's hand,
Just another lamb.

Jackie Pass

KENDAL (THE AULD GREY TOWN) AND THE LAKES

What is happening to the auld grey town?
They are pulling half of the buildings down,
The history that is around us, is disappearing too,
And very soon there will be nothing left of the old grey town to view

Buildings that have survived centuries,
That have come through wars and storms,
I don't think Henry the Eighth, would have approved,
Had he been reborn.

Wordsworth stood amongst the hills,
To view the host of daffodils,
But things would have been so different had he lived today,
Because with all the Nuclear Energy, all our daffs have died away.

The hills of peace and beauty,
Are meant for all to share,
But how can one enjoy the peace?
With low flying aircrafts there.

The world of Beatrix Potter,
Is a wondrous sight to see,
Hill top Farm, was where she sat,
Writing books for you and me.

Last of all these authors was Wainwright,
As he travelled over hills and dales,
In drawings he did the lakes captured for ever,
Knowing visitors would forget them never.

Granted we may not have all sunshine
And more often the rain comes down,
But we are the gateway to the Lakes,
And proud of this old town.

B Holme

CHIPS AND GRAVY

I've just got back to Lancashire
From a trip to London Town
They're funny folk them Cockneys - eeh!
They don't half put *us* down.
The problem is the difference
In the things we do and say
But, worst of all, they won't serve
Chips and Gravy in a tray.

It happens every single time
In every single *Cafe*
Ask for Chips and Gravy
And they call you weird or daffy.
I argue 'till my face turns blue
But just can't get my way
And have a Cockney serve me
Chips and Gravy in a tray.

Now if I get to Heaven
And St Peter's on the Door
I'll walk up to the *welcome* sign
But won't take one step more
I'll check the menu's up to scratch
Before I ring that bell
'Cos if they won't serve Chips and Gravy
Then I'd rather go to Hell.

Tommy Warburton

AROMA

Aroma means sweet fragrant smells, each has a peculiar charm,
These smells are so delicious and do no-one any harm.
The aroma of a new born babe is never quite forgotten,
Or the fresh new smell of yards and yards of pretty summer cotton.
Fragrant flowers tease the nose to soothe the savage breast,
Appetites are titillated by the smell of new baked bread.
Oh! The smell of steak and onions on an ice cold winter's day,
Or hot-pot, chips and frying fish coming down your way.
In the super modern stores the heavy scent of perfume,
Toilet soap, after shave and fresheners for our rooms.
The aromatic whiff of cigars and pipe tobacco,
Bringing memories of Christmas and Santa's heavy sacko.
Roasting meat and Yorkshire pud, coffee freshly brewed,
Tarmacadam newly spread on roads or yards and roofs.
Country smells of new mown hay, muck spreading and fat pigs,
Night scented stock, wild roses, violets and honeysuckle sprigs.
Interior smells of leather in a brand new Rolls Royce car,
Eucalyptus, Camphor oil and Vick from a smooth white jar.
Crisp firm apples, orange skins, bananas and plump strawberries,
Ozone on the fresh sea breeze, the exhaust from the ferries.
Heady bouquet of wine and sherry, brandy and liqueurs,
All to make us happy and forget our moody blues.
The deep deep breaths of cold night air as we let pussy out or in,
Can not compare with a goodnight kiss from you or her and him.

Eva Clucas

MY HUSBAND

He's a never-ending dustbin,
  always hungry, wanting more.
It's a wonder that by now
  his belly doesn't touch the floor.

His hair is short and spiky,
  like a hedgehog that is dead.
Well, that's what it looks like
  sat upon his skinny head.

His nose is on the large side;
  it sticks out a bit too far,
But it does come in useful,
  to help me open up a jar!

With a neck like an ostrich,
  and an Adam's apple too.
I have to be careful
  When I take him to the zoo.

His legs are long and spindly
  all bone without the meat.
His toes are thin and shapeless
  on barges for his feet.

He does some weight training
  to increase his muscle tones.
I don't like to tell him.
  but all you see are bones.

Although he looks so fragile
  and very thin to touch,
He knows that I really do
  Love him very much.

Mandy Parker

DREAMING OF PUSS

The unreal street that, sways in time.
The bovine feet that, trample swine.
The silken gown that, stinks of gin.
The pale hands that, let you in.
The Muscaday that, once was green.
The rising dough that, looks obscene.
The scented thighs that, roll around.
The mackerel eyes that, watch the ground.
The trembling fat that, left the bone.
The festered skull, that turned to stone.
The Diver's pearl that, never was.
The brain potato, eating, puss.
The gravy beach, the noodle pier,
The knotted sea that, groans with fear.
The stone-washed jeans that, cost too much.
The golden hand, too stiff to clutch.
The frozen creek, the tiled stream,
The broken sleep that, woke the dream.

D Flamee

J M

My daddy died when I was one
Too young to realise he was gone
I didn't have chance to shed a tear
You don't understand when only a year.

Killed when only twenty-five
I often wish he's still alive
With him to help and guide along
I know I would have grown strong.

The warmth that engulfs me when sad
I know is the spirit of you dad.

David McShane

GLORIOUS DEVON

Of all old England's counties
There is one I hold so dear,
And that is Glorious Devon
In all seasons of the year.

In Spring I see the jumping lambs
And buds burst out anew,
And from the lanes and hedgerows peep
Flowers of every hue.

In Summertime the sun shines down
From a cloudless sky,
And on every beach around the coast
One can hear the seagulls cry.

And on into the Autumn,
The wavering corn doth glow,
The farmers with their combines
To reap what they did sow.

Aye, and even in the Winter
When the landscape's stark and bare
Is there not some hidden beauty
In old Dartmoor's icy stare?

And the *Mayflower* was from Devon
As it sailed out Plymouth Sound,
With the Pilgrim Fathers
To the land Columbus found.

And then Sir Francis Drake
Playing bowls on Plymouth Hoe,
Did finish first his game
Then defeat the Spanish foe.

Was it not Sir Walter Raleigh
Yes, from Devon I'll be bound
To save his Queen from wet feet
Threw his cloak upon the ground?

In shaping England's future,
This County's done its share,
So it's *Devon, Glorious Devon*
To the folks who live down there!

David Reynolds

WOODLAND SONG

Someone sang in the woods today;
No, it wasn't a bird;
It was a clear and vibrant sound,
A trilling, thrilling, joyous round;
A carolling; no word.

The hidden songster travelled on;
No, it wasn't a bird -
Sweet cadences, with boundless ease,
Were poured among the ferny leaves;
Careless of being heard.

Then, as the singing died away;
Yes, now that's a bird;
Began the chorus loud and strong,
To carry on the joyous song,
The caroller had stirred.

So, through the leafy glade I followed on;
Yes, I saw the bird;
And felt uplifted by the glad sweet note;
The day was brighter now and cares remote;
All faith in life confirmed.

Sheila Devine

VIEW FROM THE BRIDGE

Vast panoramic splendours,
  unfold afore our eyes.
A vista full of wonders,
  each sight a new surprise.

Sweet scent of many blossoms,
  cool breath of summer breeze.
Soft music in the heavens,
  orchestrated by the trees.

The birds join in the chorus,
  a choir of tender voice.
Such beauty on a summer's day,
  so rich and vast the choice.

Small insects busy working,
  the land so green and good.
Long days of lovely memories,
  of life in Freeman's Wood.

Richard Wallbank

PLEASE LET ME IN

She looked down from her world
I looked up to her sky
Minuscule in her vision
A glint in her eye
I cried out 'How I love you'
She smiled, and then sighed
We were together, that moment
But so far apart deep inside
I tried how I've tried
But she won't let me in
To her world no-one's nowhere.
Her mind's in one endless spin
I was there for her pain
But she never notices mine
Perhaps one day she will
Perhaps one day in time
Until then I'll keep trying
To break down her wall
To get in her emotions
I'll give her my all.
You know I'm a dreamer
And I believe some dreams come true
If there's one that I hope for
It's my life here with you.

Reece Bywater

I AM

I should be ashamed my hair's not blonde
I should be ashamed my eyes aren't blue
I should be ashamed I don't wear high heels,
The adverts say so, it must be true.

I should be ashamed of not liking dresses
I should be ashamed of needing thick glasses
I should be ashamed of short legs and eye lashes
The movies are right, men don't make passes.

Why don't I try to be pretty and frilly
Why don't I try to catch a man's eye
Why won't I dress up and make up and play up
Why should I have to live any such lie.

'You won't get a husband,' who says I want one
'You won't have a family,' why should I care
'You won't have a house, a ring or a wedding'
Or end up on Valium, tearing my hair.

I won't be ashamed to be riding a rat bike
Instead of rehearsing the latest new dance
I won't be ashamed of reading James Herbert
Instead of *My Weekly* or true life romance.

I won't be ashamed that my feminine instincts
Aren't soothing some masculine ego each night
I'll be proud to be rowdy, dowdy and loudly
Stand up for myself and fight my own fight.

K M Evans

THE GOOD OLD DAYS

Whatever happened to the good old days,
When times were really hard,
When neighbours were friends,
And kids were just kids,
And you didn't have to be on your guard.
You could visit the shops,
Or go out for the day,
Without even locking your door,
You could go for a walk,
Take your kids to the park,
You can't even do that no more.
You'd call in next door, for maybe a chat,
And a friendly cup of tea,
You'd hear the new gossip, and have a good laugh,
That's just how it used to be.
But how times have changed, I'm sorry to say,
How people are just not the same,
They don't have the time, for each other no more,
They don't seem to care, what a shame.
You're not even safe in your homes anymore,
Everywhere there is locks and there's chains,
Guard dogs and alarms, to keep people out,
No wonder our life has no aims.
It's a very sad day to admit to all this,
That we'll never again feel free,
To enjoy life to the full,
Be happy and content,
In this world as it's meant to be.

Maria Farrell-Grundy

THE OLD GREY TREE

It stands upon a mound of green
The most wondrous I have ever seen
With branches strong and leaves of green
So quiet, still, as in a dream

The trunk is thick with bark so hard
In time of trouble to discard
But sad it stands there so alone
No others by it have they grown

Others look from from far away
And speak in whispers as they sway
A tale that's old but not forgot
When it was banished there to rot

Its crime no-one ever says
But it was grave in older days
In times before man did roam
And use the trees to make his home

But even man left this one alone
In it the birds did not build their home
Under its leaves no flowers grow
Just the moss that it did sow

I feel its sorrow as it stands
A warning to all the lands
Look at me I hear it say
Look at me once then turn away.

Peter Robinson

CANDLE IN THE WINDOW

Sometimes I go the long
Way home,
Over by the hill I roam,
And I stop to stare at the
House of many floors,
With its deep black windows
And creaky old doors,
But as I hurry home to tea,
An old man smiles and
Watches me,
With a sad old smile,
On his sad old face,
He looks so frail.
And out of place,
His candle in a holder,
Will burn out bright,
As he sits by the window,
Braving the night.

Lily Smith (12)

CORNERS

I miss our talks I miss your smiles
Your music sometimes drove me wild
The phone is quiet your bedroom still
No guitar sounds no boots and trainers
No washer to fill
No fry ups in the early dawn
With a hangover, sometimes you used to scorn
No running gear dropped in the hall
Sometimes I tripped over it all
Guitars, amps, music, friends, long blonde hairs
Sweaty socks thrown on the stairs
I wish you luck - from one who cared.

Patricia Flynn

THREE BALL MEN

Male golfers can be a peculiar breed
And when playing in threes they are most odd indeed
So beware all you ladies and heed what I say
Just check the first tee before starting to play

For once on the course they will not let you through
They pretend you're not there, it's a thing they all do
They've perfected the knack after many a glare
Of looking right through you, as if you're not there

We stand on the tee with our hands on our hips
And all sort of comments erupt from our lips
But they just amble along oblivious to all
They assume that the ladies just can't hit the ball

They're not all that hot at this game I conclude
And some of them can be incredibly rude
I suspect that they feel that all women should stay
At home doing housework all through the day

Yet once in the bar it is really quite strange
I see in these men a miraculous change
Hello there my dear, have you been out to play?
Yes we were behind you I pointedly say
Oh really, well if we had known it was you
We would have immediately called you on through

But I have a theory on these types of men
They have wives who give torment and fuss
So once they've escaped from the nagging old hen
They vent their frustration on us.

Barbara Trimble

FOR MY GRANDCHILDREN

'What delightful grandchildren you have,'
I hear them say
As I push the pram along the road
And blithely lead the way.
The toddlers jostle tirelessly
To hold on to my hand
And the older kids run on ahead,
We're such a happy band.
We walk and talk and skip and run,
The steepest hills we climb
And often don't get home till dark
Yet always home on time.
For time doesn't ever matter
In the memories I build,
It's just a glimpse, a state of mind
Of what, one day could be.
And all these feelings, all the joy,
Part of eternity.

Maureen Harrison Riley

CHESHIRE LINES IN FIFTY NINE

Ebony and still the night
Admire this beauty, not with sight,

Soon . . . striving waves of sound
Thrusting metallic throb and pound,

Breathed into life from pistons tight
Reach then a crescendo of glorious might,

Echoing, whirling in symphonious sound
Then gripped and swallowed by the shaking ground.

John A Harris

THE BOX

A porcelain box,
turquoise
like a pale sky;
enamelled flowers
and on the back
a gold rose
with thin writing
in French above it.

Inside is the sound of the sea;
melancholy waves
washing onto a grey shore
and silence between us;
unbreakable silence.

I could not thank you
for this fragile gift,
breathed on by someone else.

After many years
it stays on my mantelpiece;
a bleak reminder of your perfect taste
and of the icy breath of jealousy.

An anniversary present
holding a summer of pain.

Deirdre Armes Smith

SHE

She had life once
She had friends
She was the happiest,
Most carefree,
Willing of people.
She would give her all to others,
Help with no hesitation.
She was generous with her feelings
Generous with her soul.
She is suffering now
She gave too much.
She is alone
She has no friends
She has been stripped of her happiness
And her carefree world.
He hurt her
Hurt beyond belief
And so transformed
This willing and loving heart,
Into an untrusting
Tired and saddened soul
Whose salt filled tears run freely
From her reddened eyes.
Where are those she once helped?
Where are those to whom she gave her all?
They are gone
Now that she needs their generosity of heart.
Hiding, locked away in their own selfish worlds
Caring for none but themselves.
She,
She is grieving now
For the life she once had
She is distraught
She is alone.

Loren Moore

HOW LUCKY WE ARE

How lucky we are to have two feet
To help us dance to a musical beat

How lucky we are to have our toes
To balance our feet and help us pose

How lucky we are to have our heels
To help pulls and turns, how good it feels

How lucky we are to have legs that stride
They can close together or open wide

How lucky we are to have knees that bend
On how deep we go - it will depend

How lucky we are to have hips that take
The weight of each move that we make

How lucky we are to have arms to express
The way we move and compliment our dress

How lucky we are to have hands to hold
Each other close - warm or cold

How lucky we are to have a head
To turn it left, or perhaps right instead

How lucky we are to have eyes to see
Where we are going, you and me

How lucky we are to have our ears
To hear beautiful music through the years

How lucky we are to have a brain
To digest information again and again

How lucky we are to be dancing today
Thank you again - what more can I say.

Happy dancing

Julie Taylor

THE ELVES

Tiny tiny tiny were the
Little elves that played
Underneath the branches
Of the trees as they swayed
In the whooshing and swooshing
Wind that was blowing
Through the green green grass
Of the forest floor growing.

Running and jumping
Were the tiny feet that ran
Playing leap-frog and skipping
And catch-me-if-you-can
Blowing tiny trumpet horns
And dancing on the leaves
Juggling with the acorns
And chasing honey bees.

And all the leaves were dancing
As the strong wind blew
And I know I saw those elves
And I know they saw me too
But I'll never tell anyone
Where I've been today
It's a very special secret
Where the elves go out to play.

Chérianne Wren

TO THE DECLINE OF ICI'S WINNINGTON PLANT

the beast which once was so ravenous its innards grumbled day and night despite being fed in shifts is now contracting like a salted slug and spewing out hands as it goes!

Philip Johnson

PROGRESS

        Industry is slowly fading,
Shops close down through lack of trading
        Textile spinners work no more,
To lay the carpets by our door
        There's no more paper, no more steel,
No more flour mills - no big deal
        It's progress and things are a changing
Turning round and re-arranging
        We're on a winner, so one says,
But I look back on better days
When Barrow built the ocean liner,
        The Oriana, nothing finer,
Factories thrived and work was rife,
        'Twas such a cheerful, busy life
But times are hard now, jobs are few
        So what does progress do for you.

C Molloy

ESCAPE TO TATTON

When offspring's driving you insane
On long school holidays,
Transport the brats to Tatton Park
And lose them in the maze.

Now wander winding leafy paths,
Rose garden, fernery,
Then coffee-shop, indulge yourself
In cherry cake and tea.

Jenni J Moores

COUNTRY LIFE

Outsiders call us insular, unworldly or naive,
They're welcome to opinions if that's what they believe.
They've clearly never taken time to simply sit, be still
Drink in a tinkling silver brook until they've had their fill;
Or picnicked in a meadow of buttercups and clover,
Reflecting with a lover, on the day that's almost over;
Or heard the crashing, brutal force of the cruel winter sea,
Relentless, pounding angrily whilst beckoning to me;
Or chanced upon a half born lamb, whose mother loudly bleats,
As nature, playing cruel tricks, she gives birth in winter's sleet.
No not for me the city life, all dash, no time to care;
Been there, done all that, and yes I've had my share
Of smog and fumes and traffic jams, and tempers sadly frayed,
Slowly crawling home again at the end of stressful days;
But now I'm home, or as they say 'I've come back to my roots,'
Happy walking in all weathers in old green wellington boots,
Appreciating nature and living day to day,
Counting all my blessings as in my bed I lay;
Happy and contented, fulfilled and so at peace,
At one with my surroundings, at last I've found my niche.

Linda Cannings

METAMORPHOSIS

I watched them with disgusted interest
while, as a joke, they squeezed a shiny, wet refuse sack
into the hands of the submissive statue, and
(in the dogmatic insolence of their kind - everywhere)
graced his presence with a (not entirely unattractive,)
red-plastic traffic cone.
How unsurprising is this image? I thought
as the sack tightens against the wind
offsetting his crown of thorny red - plastic.
Doubling with pathetic laughter the adolescent anarchists fled.
A movement.
I look.
A figure stands, silent in the shadow.
It, like the statue, is burdened: bottle and bag.
It, like the statue, is solid and still.
It once had value too.
It once was a man.

The bottle is frozen half to his mouth.
Sadly hunched, trailing his bag on the grass
he sways gently but does not move.
I watch, then leave.
I discovered later, that they stood together for hours
forgiving, still,
rock-like in ignorance
until he was quietly arrested for defacing public property.

David Glover

TOSHIAGHT-NOA

No-one cried 'Rape' when the streets were empty once more.
Desolation followed violation and she shed a silent tear.
The child that was born of a dying passion grew like a cuckoo,
Dwarfing the land.
He paid no heed to his forefathers.

No-one cried 'Thief' as she was torn apart.
Robbed of her riches she cold only look on.
Greedy neighbours coveted her wealth,
And wormed their way into her affection.
They paid no heed to her suffering.

No-one cried 'Help' as her sister's children died.
She became fat as she was force-fed,
And longed to spew the luke-warm praise form her mouth.
She engulfed those closest to her.
Always remaining stubbornly silent.

No-one cried 'Stay' as he children left to seek their fortune.
Loneliness and isolation filled her days.
She was only cheered by the songs that floated through the empty
Valleys.
Reminding her of better days long ago.

No-one cried 'Stop' as she moved onward out of control.
They only looked on her outward beauty,
With no care for her feelings and her past they papered over the
Cracks.
Leaving her to rot from inside out.

One day they cried 'Wait' as they realised what they had done.
Rationality, nationality and patriotism broke through the barriers of
complacency.
Was it too late to operate on her gaping wounds?
Restoring her to health.

J Ayres

DANNY

I remember when I first got you
I found you in the dog's home.
You were only a pup but they'd brought you in
Beaten and starved and alone
We took you camping to Cheddar
You loved all the open space
You barked and jumped and wagged your tail
And chased us all over the place
One day my brothers went for a shower
It wasn't really that far
But you tried to follow them and got lost
You ran out and were hit by a car
We heard your howls and yelps of pain
As the coward in the car sped off
Blood was splattering everywhere
Your side was torn open, your jaw hanging off
Screaming, my mum and dad picked you up
And raced to the vet's not far away
Although we didn't have enough money with us
The vet didn't turn you away
Eight years passed since that holiday
And your mouth began to swell
The vet thought you had an abscess
But he couldn't really tell
When the x-ray came back it was bad news
You had cancer in your jaw
It was bone trauma caused by the injury
When you'd been run over years before
On my son's fourth birthday the time had come
We fought over who was to go
None of us wanted to take you to the vet's
But we all knew it had to be so

No dog could ever replace you
To us you were more than a pet
You were always part of the family
Our Danny we'll never forget.

Dawn Riccio

GOING TO SCHOOL IN OLDHAM - 1950'S STYLE

Scuffling to school through the prefabs:
Forbidden ice lolly dripping
Bright green evidence
Down clean white blouse
And yesterday's bubblegum
Traded for a look at Bunty.
Dustbin day:
Trails of potato peelings
And old newspapers
And undefined rancid smells.
Tip over the bin of
Her on the corner
And add to the growing vocabulary
Of words never to be repeated
At home.
Then the cry goes up,
'A cat! A cat!'
Fight through the crowd,
Elbow your way to the front,
Threaten the little ones,
Crawl through the legs of the big ones,
And sure enough, there's a cat:
Striped and mangy
And very, very dead

In a dustbin.

Maggie Rich

NIGHT RIDERS

There is a legend on Alderly Edge that tells of a band of sleeping warriors in a hidden cavern; they with their milk white steeds are in waiting to awake and fight a great battle against wrong. Here is my poem that tells of this awakening.

On midsummer's eve, brightly burns the wendle fire;
Awakening in the darkest cavern, the sleeping warriors rise,
With burnished swords of gold, they will this magic hour,
Ride forth on milk-white steeds and chant the battle cries.

Ride on, ride on mighty warriors,
In battle you are strong and sure,
What magic lends you strength and power,
As the flames burn bright and pure?

A full moon lights the way,
The path is straight and true,
Built in the dawning of the day
When all was bright and new.

Born of fire, you flicker and dart,
The Old Magic your strength and power,
Ride, ride on the wings of the night,
The dawn awakes within the hour.

Light glistening on sword and shield,
Swift and sure your bow, your arrow,
Mighty the power that you wield,
For this brief magic hour.

Ride on, ride on mighty warriors brave,
'Til morning creeps over the hill,
To summon you back to the grave,
So all will be peaceful and still.

Eileen Wiggins

OLD GAS LAMPS

There they stood in their regimental ways.
Those old gas lamps of yesterdays.
Posted like sentinels, with hats of glass,
With a white shrouded mantle fired by gas.
They'd arms you could swing from, where bus
Stops should be, with green flaky paint you
Could climb like a tree.

Sometimes at night would be moths round
Your head, whilst dogs, they made puddles
By cocking a leg.
Children played games out in the street, like
Tig, hop-scotch, or hide and go seek.
Boys played football, by kicking a can, or knocked
A few doors, then ran from the man, who's
Waving and shouting I'll tell your mam.

I wonder gas lamp, what tales you could tell,
Of young courting couples who stopped for
A spell, or of drunks staggering home,
From a night of good cheer, from singing
Good songs, pub games and beer.

But electric is coming, or so they say, it
Would seem your light has had its day.
Technology moves in a strange mysterious way.

I walked home thinking of these matters,
When my illuminated illusion, was to the
Pavement scattered, when this catapult stone
My dream it shatters.

I turned around to look about, but I could not
See the sling-shot lout.
For alas, it was dark. Your light was out.

Ken Mainwaring

CRIME OF FASHION

Another time, another world,
I lopped off salt and pepper curls.
Victim of this crime of fashion,
Mother cursed and swore with passion
Blamed poor Dad, and wished me dead
Then hibernated in our shed!

Betty Lightfoot

OLD LANCASHIRE

The air is chill and damp this early winter's morn,
Old Charlie the knocker up walks along the street
In cap well pulled down, in coat old and worn.
His arms aching from tap, tapping on windows
And tired his feet that tread these streets
       Every morning before five.
Gas lamps flicker, some mantels are broken,
Dogs bark, cocks crow, the village comes alive,
Clogs clatter over cobble stones,
       Good mornings are spoken.
Girls in shawls, men and boys in oily overalls
Hurry by to their work at the mill.
Five minutes to go, hooters sound
Warning them time is short, next time they boom out
They must all be ready, and willing to start.
There goes the final hooter, the engines switched on,
       The noise is terrific,
       The day's work has begun.

E Blundell

HEY YOU!

What happened to you
In your sleep
Did you get up
And did the dream end

Was this the time

You're in the paper
You're name is carved in stone
But as much as your mum tried
She couldn't bring you home

She cried
She fell, for her once lived child
She loved you so much

But being apart
Ripped you apart
It was the beginning of a start
That would end it all

The break couldn't
Come together
Through what you did

And every day we can
Wake up and smile
But it wasn't a bad dream

Hey you! What were you thinking of?

Paul Rogers

GIVE THEM THE BEAT

Give these feet the beat that's neat
Give them both a music treat
Fill each sole with joyful heat.
        Give them the beat.

Play for them on stringed guitars
Red hot notes from famous bars.
Make toes twinkle like the stars.
        Give them the beat.

Make these dogs bark happily,
Feasting on each melody.
Tapping pads in ecstasy.
        Give them the beat.

Make them jive, and make them bop
Make them never want to stop
Activate each corny crop.
        Give them the beat.

Make them roll, and make them rock,
Give them both a culture shock
Make their magic stop the clock.
        Give them the beat.

Make these heels click constantly,
As the joint jumps merrily
Teach them rockability
        Give them the beat.

Give these plates a fifties treat
Sprinkle spice upon the meat.
Make these dragsters super fleet.
        Give them the beat.

Violet M Corlett

MI JOINERY

Family skills are handed down,
They say, from sire to son,
So, if Daddy Bill had certain skill -
So had little John.

Now a name-sake of mine on the family line,
At joinery, was good,
With such a flair, could make a chair
Out o' any piece o' wood.

But come what may, I don't display,
The craftsmanship he knew,
For I always fail, to hit the nail,
And I cannot saw or screw.

I thought I would use up some wood,
To make a garden seat,
All workmanlike and stable,
And rigid, firm and neat.

When I had done, I sat upon, the seat as best I could,
But I gave a cough, and the legs fell off,
And I sat down in the mud.

When she heard me shout, the wife came out,
And in sympathy, she said,
'With luck perhaps, you can use the scraps
For duck-boards in your shed!'

John Fearn

THE REMEDY

So,
you got it all worked out?
What
when
where
with who?
Cosy,
you got it all wrapped up
shiny paper
ribbons
bows
your whole life
gift wrapped
a perfect fit
a pair of well worn
dog chewed slippers?
Boring!

The remedy?
Take a slice
of real life
savour
the flavour
repeat daily
best taken before
death.

Louise Hamilton

POVERTY IS UGLY SON

Looking through old photographs
Of family and friends
I had to smile at the changes
Wrought in fashion trends
Especially school photos my -
What a sight we looked
Shaven heads *for the nits*
Cut down father's trousers
We really were the pits
But what stories could be told
Of poverty and strife
We children weren't to blame
For how we looked, that was our life
My son who's never known the hunger
That I've known
Remarked how ugly all the children looked
Not like the ones today
With bonny faces and well dressed
And stomachs that are full
I closed my album on the past
And answered with a sigh
I pray they will never know bad times
Just prosperity health and fun
And things to always stay that way
For it's poverty that is ugly Son.

H Warburton

AT A LANCASHIRE STATION

Well, he sat at Lime Street Station
    Up in the White Star Bar.
Watched the comings and the goings
    Saw the people from afar.

There were families from Lancashire, returning to their home.
    A group of priests all eager as they set out for Rome.
There came a throng of Japanese, the Cavern Club to see.
A bunch of Spanish sailors, heading back towards the quay.

The baggage was so colourful, rucksacks of every hue.
    But here and there a cardboard box,
A parcel wrapped in haste -
    Mingles with brown leather
For those with wealth and taste.

He sipped his beer then noticed the kissing it had stopped,
    For everyone was looking at the huge old station clock.
This masterpiece from Shropshire relentlessly moves on
    To remind all those below, it is time that they were gone.

Rod Nightingale

JUST ANOTHER COUNCIL ESTATE

This street is full of hopes
based on bets and football teams
pop stars and cinemas and drink
These homes are full of luxuries
which the people display proudly
trying to prove that they do not
really belong here
Brimming with children and scandal
everyone returns to the bed
aftermath of the pub

They live from debt to debt
between the weekly wage
and the latest social benefit
The angry now join action groups
the old complain condone vote
and then abuse their candidate

They still believe in people
they have never met
and their part will end
at the ballot box
for those who bother still to vote

This street is full of dope
injected bets and football teams
pop stars and cinemas and drink

Stephen Starkie

HOLIDAY PACKING

I wonder if the weather will be warm or cold
My new girdle makes me look so slim
But I'll be more comfy in the old,
I'll take along some jumpers and cardigans too
A summer dress, cool blouses, and a skirt or two,
Underclothes, night-clothes, mirror and a comb.
Raincoat and umbrella, oh there's so many things I
                      wish I was coming home.
I wish I was like the young ones
The young ones in their teens
And take a couple of jumpers and just a pair of jeans,
My luggage is too heavy for me to carry about
So let's get it open again, and see what I can do without.

K Leigh

THE JUMPER

Mi aunty lived in Wigan
It were a gradely town,
She knitted me a jumper
Purple, green and brown.

Like most Lancashire lassies
She were noted for her thrift,
So, she used old balls of wool up
To make this colourful gift.

Seems somethin' must have gone all wrong
For the body were a squeeze,
And the sleeves were just a shade too long
'Cos they came down past mi knees.

While her needles were a clickin'
And her wool were runnin' slack,
She dropped the odd stitch here and there
But didn't put 'em back.

Still, it had its compensations
Even though it were all rough,
On winter nights I put it on
And tucked mi feet inside the cuffs.

Lancashire folk aren't mean you know
Just careful with their brass,
And mi Aunty, though she couldn't knit
Were a canny Lancashire lass.

Edith

HORWICH CARNIVAL PROCESSION

Horwich Carnival Procession
Comes but once a year,
But when it travels down our streets
It brings with it much cheer.
With brass bands booming out their tunes
And horses clopping by,
Proud mothers watch their rosebuds
As they blossom, heads held high.
Clog-dancers and pretty girls
Add motion to the movement,
As elven beings collect pennies
To help pay for improvement.
Local businesses are represented
By each float;
Each one of them so picturesque,
It makes each person gloat
Upon each moving work of art,
A kingdom in itself;
Each one striving to be best,
Not to be on the shelf.
Yes, the carnival is something
We look forward to,
And as it travels down our streets
It stops us feeling blue.

Jackie Elvy

A NOSTALGIC RETURN TO A LANCASHIRE DALE

After many years away, returning once again
Deepdale had retained its charm
It never seems to wane

Elegant still the stone houses
Almost a Georgian air
No longer though the formal shops
We used when I lived there

Now there are gaudy posters
Where once Miss Allandale served her dainty cakes on crystal stands
Where gossip and news was heard
No longer the trams do clatter up and down the hill
You cannot hear the sound of the bell or the click clack click of the till

You can still look down the dale though and up to Beacon Fell
When the bus stops at St Stephen's Road if a passenger pushes the bell

'Pop in Ere and Byem' forever keeps its name
Even the Station though minus the trains
Looks very much the same

All is very different though
The people I knew are gone
Only memories of my Deepdale
Forever linger on.

Bunty Aldred

TRIATHLON - THE BIKE

Wetsuit unzipped, dangles from the waist. Tired
bodies forced to sprint to waiting bikes.
A rain dance follows, shedding suit like
unwanted skin, helmet on, shoes on, many times
rehearsed but now, in nervous tension, all fingers
and thumbs. Numbed feet search for reluctant
pedals and at last the ride begins.

A fleeting chill on damp bodies, soon forgotten
in heat of battle. Curled like downhill skiers,
fighting wind and road, legs pumping pedals, eyes
locked ahead, fatigue lost in mesmerised concentration,
pain like the passing countryside, always there but
ignored. Time, as always is the enemy.

Soon the final miles beckon, heart and mind
lifted for those final minutes. Untapped reserves
released in an elated burst of energy to cross the
line. Cycles racked, running shoes on wooden
feet, and legs, now unwilling, somehow begin the
run.

Robert Keith

THE RAILWAY WORKER

A fantasy job from young up to old.
Working with trains enormous and bold.
Electrics, diesels, steamers of past.
All British made and built to last.
The railtracks they run on, need constant care.
Length walkers taking notes, for plate layers
to repair.
Worn tracks, damaged sleepers,
keys out of chairs.
Plenty of work, for rail gangs that care.
Never a dull moment from one day to next.
Seven days a week, not getting much rest.
All through the Summer months.
Burnt to a cinder,
blisters on the backs, segs on the fingers.
Then Winter draws in, cold and dark,
but they work all the time.
Never making a bark
    Oh to be a railway worker!

Steven Bennett Whiteley

NA-LAD

As ye walking down them cobble stowans,
All spit and polish we clogs a glowen.
As I passed owd wass, donkey stowan
In one hand, scrubbing brush in other
A cleaning them owd Joe stones until
All spick and span and a glowan, a ses
By gum lass you're a good un,
      As old Tom passed on is hos and cart
A shating a rag a rag bowen, four jam jars
For a donkey stowan.
      One man stopped us saying where
Does ti come from lad, I ses a come
From owd cotton mill in there Lancashire
Where does ti think a come from, not them
Posh places down Sowath.
      He said na lad I should a noan
Ye Lancashire through and through
Get kettle on the arth he sen, and
We'll both have a good pot a ta and a
Jam butty, make sure the poke fire
Fost as they chill goes right to ye
Bones as ye walking down ye cobble
Stowans.

H W Fogarty

THE SHADOW

They hear me but don't listen
They look but don't see me
I don't recognise the person
That they have made of me.

I live with many people
But I am quite alone
As solid as a shadow
Made out of skin and bone.

This is my home but I am lost
Complete my self-destruction
Safe in my terraced prison
Made of my own construction.

Tears are my close companions
Although they seldom show
A smile that doesn't reach my eyes
A heart as cold as snow.

I played the part I thought was mine
Suppressed what made me me
And now I am a shadow
Of what I was meant to be.

Anne Cooper-Halton

SPELLBOUND . . .

High on Alderley's highest point I made a wish so long ago
It was a dream so distant then but one I held too closely
I looked beyond the hills and far beyond the skyline
Eighteen . . . the world is at my feet and yet it is so far.

Castle Rock . . . Castle Rock . . . you have seen so much
Lovers come and lovers go but you remain steadfast
You take the ice of winter's chill and summer's burning sun
You know that life's not easy you know it all too well.

The woods surround you, fall beneath you
Praying in the wind . . .
Owls hoot with darkness as birdsong slowly dies
Don't come on Halloween . . . no no. . . Come in the spring . . .

Then come and make your wish and whisper to the wind
Tell it to the springtime sky as the leaves unfurl
Then my child . . . leave your echoes to the gentle breeze
Wait you must - but that's the game we all have to play.

Jean Carter

JOE AND STEPH

Bonded were they that night
Beneath the hospital lights
Both suffering similar pain
Only one saw light of day again.

Joe and Steph
Had chose to die
Nurses, doctors sought
To save a lie

Steph, don't hide the tears you cry
We know how you felt when he had to die
You got life and he got death
There's nothing fair about that Steph

Steph and Joe
Bonded so,
Then torn asunder
Her life a victory
His death a blunder

Stephie, Stephie,
Don't cry so,
Don't cry 'cos of
What happened to Joe
He died as he chose to do
Life, you didn't choose
Was forced on you
You wanted death as well
Now he goes to heaven
And you're trapped in hell

Catherine Makin

A VICTIM OF THE ARMENIAN EARTHQUAKE

The earth came down with a mighty roar.
There was no hint of it before.
A sudden, swirling, soggy mass
That choked and stifled, caused life to pass.

We felt all alone and dazed
Our bodies changed, we were amazed.
We did not know where we had come;
It seemed so far removed from home.

We seemed to travel very far
There was no light - not even a star,
It was misty - where should we go?
We moved about - just to and fro!

Suddenly the mist did clear
There were people saying 'Come over here'
They led us to a peaceful place
They were kind and good and full of grace.

I would like to see my mum.
I do not think that she has come.
They tell me I shall see her when
The time has come, and not 'til then.

It's very safe and lovely here.
I have not anything to fear.
I'll do as they say and try my best
To be calm and tranquil and rest.

Joan Williams

WASTWATER

Fiercely
a golden sun
shrivelled the day.
By the dry bones
of the screes
the water lay
still,
deep,
cold,
guarding the ice
in its soul

Shelly Tomlinson

MYSTIC MEG ON THE LOTTERY SHOW

Memory, a geyser gushing
From pram to present,
Reliably reminds one
Of those selected highlights
Of a life so far lived.
Take me now, pace Mystic Meg,
Forward to the future:
Must this be little lapses,
Spiralling decay and death?

Smack! Splash!
Earth falls like rain
On my coffin lid,
Muffled voices murmur
Incantations, footfalls shuffle
On damp gravel and someone
Drops a key upon my head.

No! Stay now where the light
Turns inward, and water
Runs on cold stones;
Here is lush lilac
And cool, clean fingers
Interlaced with youthful bones.
Curtains swish through
Warm windows, and, when you sleep,
Your modern dreams are sweet.

Deborah Casson

FREEDOM

Galloping in the sun,
Being led by fun.
The hills coming closer,
Beautiful, high and cool.
Galloping the majestic stallion
Outruns us all.
Tails flowing behind us.
Manes blowing in the strong breeze.
Our foals eager to keep up.
Knowing we are free to do as we please.
Not kept in stables and doing as we are told.

One day some men came, and rounded us up
We fought and kicked,
But it did no good.
They made us board a truck,
And took us to a market where they sold us
                one by one.

A man bought and took me home,
I missed my foal.
He trained me to be ridden by his daughter
Today I live in a stable,
Longing for my free life galloping in the hills.

Julia Yates

THE FIDELITY OF FAITH

May our principles and fidelity still remain high!
That purer faith in relationships which can trust
Without question: knowing that what is said
And done is just true!

Won't it be great when all pretence is swept away
That we *get* what we see feel and sense in a person
Facing that facet of us called God: As we are
Stretched, tested, strengthened renewed and finally
Ultimately purified as He wishes us to be -
Or not? - That is the answer!

When we arrive there really doesn't matter
Providing we keep that Hope-Faith belief
In the all true one God of conditionless Love:
Whether one ideal is married to another
Or whether singly it develops into ethos.

But then again we must guard against
That falling away; as of talents;
Dust-gathering, festering, hankering, rusting
So *please* beware His dead wood stage of vine branch pruning.
Into the fire of misuse of this world's excuses disuse:
By harnessing our gifts to selfless, earthly good-deed use,
As our Father would rather we upstore heavenly treasure.

The main point of thrust though must
Be Honesty's open non-adulterous truth
Able to be trusted unto death during life;
One person's tryst to another until relations end.

A one-lover monogamy
During that time in life
Until in changeover terms, sharing
We all become birdlike, free;
To choose who and where we are,
What we think, say and do in love and liberty:
And with whom we are to be
Emotionally, spiritually for ever free.

Mack A Duerden

KIDS TODAY

'I don't know,' we seem to say,
What's the matter with kids today,
There is a problem we cannot deny,
That surely begins with you and with I
What's right is right! What's wrong is wrong!
We must adhere to the same old song
Times are changing as years go by
Walloping of children does not now apply
It used to be the short sharp smack
Which ended in tears, it will come back
Ever so simple, so brief, so quick.
Magic in discipline, it did do the trick
We must sit and talk social workers do say
Conversant in words that end in dismay
We hear, as well and as good we do,
We read psychiatry, psychology too,
Enough is enough, the decision is here,
Is it verbal chastisement or a slap on the ear.

Bert Horsley

CHILDHOOD DREAMS

Lying in bed
Coat tucked under my chin
Waiting silently in the dark
Listening for dad to come in.

The front door slams
My heart skips a beat
Tap, tap on the oil cloth
Made by his feet.

I crouch up closer
To my sister in the dark
I know she's awake
Like me
Waiting for dad to start.

It doesn't take long
His angry shouts
Mam's frightened scream
I put my fist to my eyes
Trying to rub away the dream.

Sneaking out of bed
Mam's sat on the stairs
Sobbing gently
Hands in her hair.

Come up Mam
I whisper urgently
We'd protect her
My sister and me.

She shook her head
Ordered me back to bed
Morning came
Nothing again, is said.

Emma Shaw

THE DERBYSHIRE DIET!

In this day of diets,
Of healthy new cuisine,
Non toxic drinks and foot to eat
So we're all fit and lean!

When hunger pangs are quieted
By an apple, rosy red
And low fat spread is thinly applied
On wholesome, wholemeal bread,

What better can you ask for
Than a plate of meat and veg?
Fluffy Yorkshire pudding,
Gravy running off the edge!

A steaming mug of *toxic* tea
A plate of bread and butter,
Syrup sponge for pudding,
Creamy custard . . . makes hearts flutter!

A really full chip butty,
Cooked in dripping, real and fat!
With lots of butter on soft bread . . .
No lumps of grain in that!

A tasty chop, with crispy fat,
Baked spuds with lots of cheese!
Fresh green veg and carrots,
And the palate will be pleased!

Not a taste of saccharin,
Nor a grain stuck in the teeth!
It never killed our Grannies
And our tummies get relief!

S Williamson

DON'T JUDGE A BOOK . . .

If she could be someone else,
My friend said that she would be me,
But the qualities which she admires,
Are not all of me.

Behind the laughing eyes,
And the ever present smile,
There lies the tears and pain,
Which I have suffered for a while.

Cool and confident, she said,
No-one will ever know,
How I really feel,
Unless I tell them so.

Self-sufficient and courageous,
Just look deep into my eyes,
All the things that she sees,
Are just a good disguise.

Inside this human body,
There beats a battered heart,
Too scared to take a risk,
Or chance being ripped apart.

You should not envy another's personality,
Nor the way they look,
Because whilst the cover seems appealing,
You may not like to read the book.

Marianne Pilkington

XMAS LAMENT

It would be about October when I first evolved the plan
That instead of wine and soap and socks,
I'd browse around for hours in little giftie shops,
I'd choose with care and insight, gifts for every taste
Not like my usual shopping sprees, grabbing everything in haste.

This year, the Xmas cake, will not be iced still warm,
No this year will be different, I will make it weeks before,
I'll wrap it well and store it and let it all mature
It will be the very best of cakes of that you can be sure.
I'll make lots and lots of mince pies all of which I'll freeze,
Oh to be so organised no last minute rush for me.

I'll do my Xmas cleaning everything pristine,
I'll wash and dust and polish, nothing will I leave.
There will not be a cobweb nor a speck of dust in sight,
How glad I am I made this plan, I think I'll start tonight.

October seemed to go so fast but yet I've time to spare
I've got my list of do's and don'ts tomorrow I'll prepare.

You couldn't win now could you, I went and got the 'flu,
November's been and now has gone, the robin sings December's song
There's still time three weeks to go, I'll start running in a day or so.

Just days to go I'm on the hop, no time for little giftie shops
But soap and socks and gifts of wine are very nice for friends of mine.
The cake and mince pies sad to say, that plan I had fell by the way.
I'll buy them in for who's to care, they'll never notice on Xmas day.
As for cleaning you can guess, I'm still in my usual mess.
Spiders rampant but how can I kill, is this not the time for peace and
goodwill.

It is Xmas day already and I give a little sigh
Thinking of the plans I had that seemed to go awry
But next year will be different, I'll make my list quite soon
Perhaps I'll plan the Xmas rush in the early part of June.

Clare Martin

INFORMATION

We hope you have enjoyed reading this book - and that you will continue to enjoy it in the coming years.

If you like reading and writing poetry drop us a line, or give us a call, and we'll send you a free information pack.

Write to

>Anchor Books Information
>1-2 Wainman Road
>Woodston
>Peterborough
>PE2 7BU